EASY EMBELLISHMENTS
FOR CREATIVE SEWING™

Edited by Barbara Weiland

HOUSE of
WHITE
BIRCHES

PUBLISHERS
SINCE 1947

Easy Embellishments for Creative Sewing™

Copyright © 2007 House of White Birches, Berne, Indiana 46711

EDITOR	Barbara Weiland
ART DIRECTOR	Brad Snow
PUBLISHING SERVICES DIRECTOR	Brenda Gallmeyer
ASSOCIATE EDITOR	Dianne Schmidt
ASSISTANT ART DIRECTOR	Nick Pierce
COPY SUPERVISOR	Michelle Beck
COPY EDITORS	Nicki Lehman, Mary O'Donnell
GRAPHIC ARTS SUPERVISOR	Ronda Bechinski
BOOK DESIGN	Amy S. Lin
GRAPHIC ARTISTS	Glenda Chamberlain, Edith Teegarden
PRODUCTION ASSISTANTS	Marj Morgan, Judy Neuenschwander
TECHNICAL ARTIST	Nicole Gage
PHOTOGRAPHY	Tammy Christian, Don Clark, Matthew Owen, Jackie Schaffel
PHOTO STYLISTS	Tammy Nussbaum, Tammy M. Smith
CHIEF EXECUTIVE OFFICER	David J. McKee
MARKETING DIRECTOR	Dan Fink

Printed in China
First Printing: 2007
Library of Congress Control Number: 2006928193
Hardcover ISBN: 978-1-59217-152-1
Softcover ISBN: 978-1-59217-175-0

1 2 3 4 5 6 7 8 9

Contents

Welcome!

Get ready for a fabulous sewing experience that will expand your creativity and enhance your skills. *Easy Embellishments for Creative Sewing* is chock-a-block full of terrific techniques for creating one-of-a-kind garments, accessories and home decor items that will surely turn heads.

Embellishments and decorative details set special sewing projects aside from the ordinary. Now you can learn myriad ways to jazz up your sewing projects for added style and panache. Embroidery, embossing, patchwork, appliqué, faux chenille, stamping, stenciling, painting, felting and beading—these techniques, featured in the following pages, are only a few of the wonderful ways to express yourself in fabric.

Perhaps you've yearned to try beading or embossing but didn't know where to start. Or, you've admired appliquéd garments enhanced with beads, crystals or embroidery. Or patchwork intrigues you, but you need a jump-start to help you plan a great garment. As you look through the pages in this exciting book, you'll find inspiration along with step-by-step directions for embellishing and enhancing your favorite project. Color photos and illustrations make it easy to try something new while you sew something special. Inspiration is at your fingertips in this exciting book with great projects and lots of color photos and how-to illustrations to help you enhance skills you already have or add new ones to your creative sewing toolbox.

Before you begin, grab a few bookmarks or sticky notes to tag the projects and techniques that you want to try. I'm sure you'll find more than one that appeals to your sense of style and your sewing skills. Have a great time in your sewing room!

Warm regards,

Barbara

Embellishments

Ordinary to extraordinary—that's what happens when you enhance
the fabric surface with stitching, beading, stamping, painting, foiling,
piping, embroidery or fused confetti. Create interest, texture
and excitement with these fun embellishing techniques.

ALPHABET SOUP

Design by Lucy B. Gray

Remember trying to spell out your name in a bowl of alphabet soup? With stamped letters floating out of the appliquéd soup bowls on this reversible vest, you can spell anything you want! Paint your own fabric following the directions below, or use colored tone-on-tone prints for the vest and vest lining if you prefer. The fun is in learning how to make and apply your own letter stamps using simple materials and fabric paints.

Finished Size
Your size

Techniques
Fabric painting
Stamping on fabric
Fusible appliqué

Materials
• Vest pattern of your choice, without darts, facings or a center-back seam
• 2½ yards bleached muslin, preshrunk
• ⅔ yard purple gingham check fabric (or a shirt from the thrift store)
• ¾–1 yard lightweight fusible knit, woven or weft-insertion interfacing (enough for 2 vest fronts and 1 vest back)
• ⅛ yard purple calico fabric
• ⅛ yard yellow calico fabric
• All-purpose thread to match fabrics
• White or natural pearl cotton thread
• Paper-backed fusible web
• Air- or water-soluble marking pen
• 3 pieces sheet foam (from the craft store)
• 3 sheets clear acetate (for making transparencies)

- Fabric paints in yellow, gold, white and purple (plus related colors, if desired)
- All-purpose craft glue
- Foam and artist paintbrushes
- Fine craft scissors
- Regular craft scissors
- *Optional:* brayer
- Paper towels
- Scrap paper and pencil
- Small plastic cups for holding paints
- Plastic plate for mixing paints
- Resealable plastic bag
- Cotton-tipped applicators
- Old towel
- Plastic shower curtain or other plastic sheet to protect work surface
- Computer and printer
- Word processing software with different fonts
- Iron and press cloth
- Rotary cutter, mat and ruler
- Basic sewing tools and equipment

Cutting

- Adjust the vest front and back pattern pieces to accommodate your size and shape as needed.
- Cut away the armhole seam allowances and the neckline and front-edge and bottom-edge seam allowances to prepare the edges for the bound-edge finish.
- Cut oversized muslin rectangles large enough to accommodate the pattern pieces (two left fronts, two right fronts and two full back pieces). Trace the vest shapes on the rectangles with a pencil.
- Use the front pattern to cut one right and one left front from the fusible interfacing. Cut one back from the interfacing.
- Cut two 6 x 20-inch pieces of preshrunk muslin for the soup bowls.
- Cut enough 1⅞-inch-wide bias strips from the gingham check fabric to make four yards of binding after sewing the strips together with bias seams.
- Trace three soup bowls (page 12) onto paper. Trace one soup bowl inside onto paper. Cut out.

Making the Sheet-Foam Stamps

1. Using your computer's word processor, create a file with selected alphabet letters, size 72 points, in your choice of font (Bookman Old Style shown in sample). Some letters make more of a visual impact, like "g" and "y," so consider the aesthetics of each letter's shape when selecting them. Enlarge the letters to range in size from 1½–6 inches tall and print one copy of each, using either photo-editing software or a photocopier.

2. Use fine craft scissors to cut out the paper letters, leaving narrow borders around each one. Coat the wrong side of each letter with all-purpose craft glue and mount onto foam sheets. Place the foam pieces under heavy books for at least 30 minutes to allow the glue to set.

3. After the glue has dried, cut out each letter using fine craft scissors. Coat the paper sides of the letters with craft glue and mount them onto similar-sized pieces cut from the acetate sheets. Place the stamps under the books again and allow to dry for several hours (Photo 1).

Photo 1

Painting & Assembly

Note: *It can take two days and a dedicated worktable to paint all the components for this vest, but the results will be well worth the wait!*

1. Place an old shower curtain or plastic sheet on your worktable. For the vest's yellow side, dampen one left and one right front muslin piece and one back piece and arrange them, right side up, on the plastic.

2. Pour enough yellow paint into a small plastic cup to cover the bottom, and dilute it with an equal amount of water. Dilute other colors in the same way. Remix fresh paint as needed. Using a foam brush, paint the three vest pieces, trying for a blotchy, uneven effect.

3. On a plastic plate, mix a tiny amount of purple with diluted yellow to create a diluted warm brown, and dab it here and there on the pieces with a wet paper towel. With the artist's brush, paint a wavy grid in diluted purple across the three pieces. Soak a wet paper towel in very diluted brown and squeeze it out over the pieces to create the look of soup stains (Photo 2).

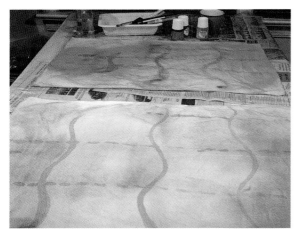

Photo 2

4. Use the soup bowl template as a size guide and paint three slightly oversized yellow bowl shapes onto one of the 6 x 20-inch muslin rectangles (Photo 3). If desired, use other colors, such as orange or brown, to create a shadowed effect. Allow all the painted pieces to dry overnight. If you have another protected surface, move the yellow pieces there to dry, and continue painting. Wipe off the plastic sheet before painting the purple pieces.

Photo 3

5. Repeat steps 2–4 to paint the purple pieces (substituting purple paint for yellow). This time paint the wavy grids in darker purple, and make the soup splotches with some diluted yellow (Photo 4).

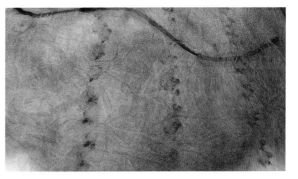

Photo 4

6. Use the soup bowl template as a guide to paint three purple bowl shapes on the remaining 6 x 20-inch piece of muslin. Allow all the painted pieces to dry overnight.

7. Place the three yellow vest pieces right side up on an old towel. Pin the paper soup bowl templates in their proper positions, and arrange the letter stamps right side up so they appear to stream out of the bowls in a wavy pattern.

8. When you are pleased with the arrangement, lift each stamp, one by one, and use an artist's brush to paint the wrong side with undiluted purple fabric paint. If available, roll a brayer over the stamp to distribute the paint more evenly. Press the stamp firmly in place on the vest piece. Lift the stamp, and continue in this manner until you have stamped each of the letters. Remove any paint blobs in the crevices of the stamp with a cotton-tipped applicator. Touch up any letters with an artist's brush, if desired. To add more texture to the design, print some of the letters a second time without repainting. Rinse the brush and stamps in water after printing, but don't soak the stamps—the foam letters may come off!

9. Repeat steps 7 and 8 with the purple vest pieces. This time, mix some gold paint with yellow and white for stamping (Photo 5).

Photo 5

10. Allow several hours for the stamped letters to dry. Heat-set the paints by sandwiching each vest piece between two pieces of scrap muslin and pressing it on the wrong side. Use the hottest setting and no steam, and press each painted area several times for short periods to avoid scorching. You can also place the pieces in a dryer and tumble on the highest setting for 10 minutes. Check frequently to avoid overheating both the dryer and the fabric!

11. Place three yards of white or natural pearl cotton in a resealable plastic bag with diluted purple paint. Allow several minutes for the paint to penetrate the pearl cotton fibers, and then remove and place between several layers of paper towels. Press out

the excess paint and sandwich pearl cotton between fresh paper towels. Steam the pearl cotton with the iron for a minute to set the color, and then rinse under water to ensure that it won't bleed later on; allow to dry thoroughly (Photo 6).

Photo 6

12. Use the bowl template to cut three soup bowls each from the yellow and purple painted muslin. Using the paper pattern, cut three bowl insides each from the yellow and purple calico fabrics. Cut and apply fusible web to the wrong side of each bowl and each bowl inside following the manufacturer's directions. Remove the backing paper.

13. Position the bowl insides on the vest fronts and backs (yellow to purple and purple to yellow), and then overlap a soup bowl on each one. Fuse in place following the manufacturer's directions. Using the air- or water-soluble marking pen, draw three wavy "steam" lines from the rim of each bowl.

14. Use the purple pearl cotton thread to do running stitches along each steam line on the yellow vest pieces (Photo 7). Use unpainted pearl cotton to stitch the steam lines on the purple side of the vest.

Photo 7

Figure 1
Pin and sew gingham binding to vest,
beginning at lower edge of vest back.

19. Turn the binding over the raw edge to the purple side. Turn the binding raw edge under along the stitching and press. Slipstitch the binding in place.

20. Bind the armholes in the same manner, beginning and ending the binding in the underarm area, but not right at the side seams, to avoid unnecessary bulk. Make sure the stitches catch only the purple vest so they don't show on the yellow side. ❖

15. Cut each vest piece from the painted muslin along the drawn lines—or replace the vest pattern, pin in place and cut out. Apply the fusible interfacing to the wrong side of each of the three purple vest pieces following the manufacturer's directions.

16. Sew the shoulder and side seams of the yellow vest and press the seams open. Repeat with the purple vest pieces. Trim the seam allowances in the purple vest to ⅜ inch wide to eliminate bulk.

17. With wrong sides together and seams aligned, smooth the two vests together. Note that the vests may not be precisely the same size due to cutting discrepancies. That's OK. What's most important is that the layers are smooth and wrinkle-free. If one side extends beyond the other, don't worry about it as long as the difference is not greater than ⅜ inch. Should the difference exceed that, trim it to ⅜ inch. Machine-baste around the armholes and unfinished edges. Check again to make sure there are no wrinkles or pulls and adjust if necessary by undoing the stitching and then basting again.

18. Turn under and press ¼ inch at one short end of the gingham check binding strip. Beginning at the bottom edge of the vest back, pin the binding to the yellow side of the vest with raw edges even. When you reach the turned end, overlap the binding and trim the excess. Stitch ⅜ inch from the raw edges (Figure 1).

Foiling With Stamps

Try embellishing beautiful purchased fabrics with foiled designs using your sheet-foam stamps! Go one step further by making stamps from not just letters, but other symbols hiding in your word processor. For example, I found this neat symbol ◞ in the Wingdings 2 font of Microsoft Word (Type "g") and foiled it onto a lovely polyester print. Let your imagination soar while wandering through these offbeat font libraries!

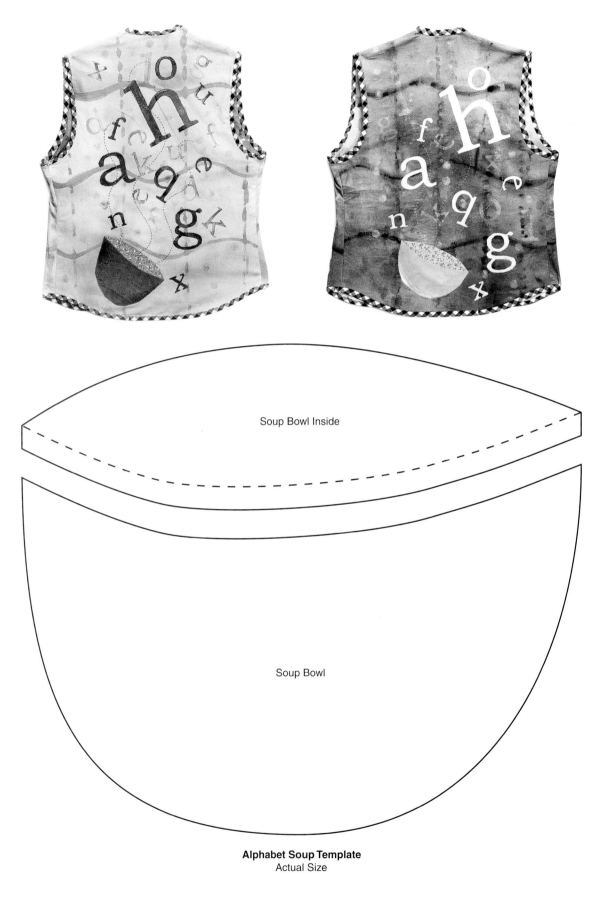

Soup Bowl Inside

Soup Bowl

Alphabet Soup Template
Actual Size

BEADED SHRUG

Design by Stephanie Corina Goddard

Beading and couching add style and visual punch to the front panels of this comfortable little wrap made from rectangles.

Finished Sizes
Small, medium and large

Techniques
Beading
Couching

Materials
Project Note: *Consider a busy print to mask the stitching lines that hold the narrow facings in place, or be sure to choose a closely matched thread color. The contrast fabric yardage given is for panels cut on the crosswise grain.*
- 44/45-inch-wide fabric for the shrug
    Small: 2 yards
    Medium or Large: 2¼ yards
    ¼ yard contrast for front panels
- All-purpose thread to match fabrics
- Clover Mini Quick Fusible Bias Tape or flexible braid trim or decorative yarn for couched design (also see Optional Embellishments on page 17)
- Assorted beads
- Chalk pen or dressmaker's chalk
- Basic sewing tools and equipment

Cutting
- From the main fabric, cut one rectangle for the size you are making.
    Small: 28½ x 72 inches
    Medium: 30 x 75 inches
    Large: 31½ x 78 inches
- For all sizes, cut two 2-inch-wide facing strips along the lengthwise grain of the remaining main fabric.
- From the contrast fabric, cut two front panel rectangles for the size you are making.
    Small: 9 x 19 inches
    Medium: 9 x 21½ inches
    Large: 9 x 22 inches

Assembly

Project Note: *Use ¼-inch-wide seam allowances.*

1. With wrong sides together and long raw edges even, fold each front panel in half; press a crease along the fold. Place the panels side by side with folds at center. Trim away a wedge at the lower end of each panel (Figure 1).

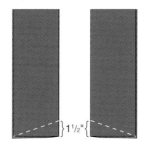

Figure 1
Trim away wedge at lower
end of each folded panel.

2. Open each panel and embellish with couching and beading as desired (also see Optional Embellishments on page 17). Use a chalk pen or dressmaker's chalk to draw meandering lines for the couched trim. Fuse mini bias in place following the manufacturer's directions, or stitch flexible braid trim or decorative yarn in place by hand or machine as desired. Add beaded accents. Note that the embellishments on the two panels shown are not identical (Figure 2).

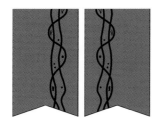

Figure 2
Embellish the front panels as desired.

3. With right sides together, fold each panel in half and stitch ¼ inch from the short angled end (Figure 3). Trim the pointed corner at a diagonal and turn each panel right side out. Press carefully and machine-baste ¼ inch from the long edges.

Figure 3
Fold front panels in half with right sides
facing. Stitch ¼" from lower angled end.

4. Position the front panels on the right side of the large rectangle for the shrug with raw edges aligned. Machine-baste in place. Fold one of the 2-inch-wide facing strips in half with wrong sides facing and long edges aligned and press. With raw edges even, pin the folded facing strip to the panel and trim away any excess. Stitch ¼ inch from the raw edges (Figure 4).

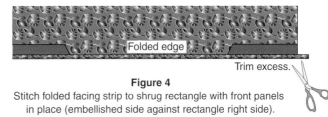

Figure 4
Stitch folded facing strip to shrug rectangle with front panels
in place (embellished side against rectangle right side).

5. Turn the facing to the wrong side with the front panels extending toward each other and press. Pin the facings in place and stitch close to the folded edge (Figure 5).

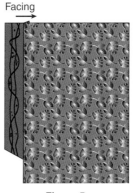

Figure 5
Turn facing to inside,
press and stitch in place.

6. Fold one end of the large rectangle to meet the opposite long edge as shown in Figure 6. Repeat with the opposite end. Beginning at the neckline, pin toward each short end, ending approximately 6 inches from the triangle point for the wrist opening. Stitch as pinned, backstitching at the front panels but not at the wrist edges.

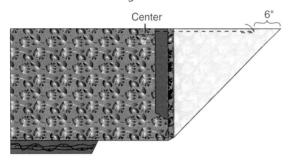

Figure 6
Fold panel end up and stitch to within 6"
of the point. Repeat with remaining end.

7. Try on the shrug and mark the desired finished sleeve length with a pin. Remove and draw a cutting line ¼ inch past the pin to allow for the facing seam allowance. Cut on the line (Figure 7).

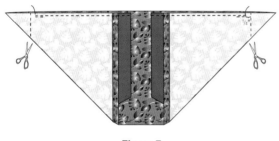

Figure 7
Trim excess at each point to desired length;
allow for ¼"-wide facing seam allowance.

8. Serge- or zigzag-finish the shoulder seam allowances together and press toward the back of the shrug.

9. Adjust the sewing machine for a shorter-than-average stitch length. Stitch ¼ inch from the raw edge for 1 inch on each side of the V at the lower edge of each wrist opening. Clip to, but not past the stitching (Figure 8).

Figure 8
Reinforce the lower edge of the
wrist opening. Clip to stitching.

10. Measure the distance around the wrist opening edge and add 2 inches. Cut two sleeve facings this length from the remaining 2-inch-wide facing strip. Fold in half lengthwise with wrong sides facing and press.

11. Pin a facing strip to the right side of each sleeve opening edge with 1 inch extending at each end. Beginning and ending at the point of the clipped V, stitch ¼ inch from the raw edges. Mark the stitching line along the lower edge of the sleeve on the facing extensions and trim the excess ¼ inch from the marking (Figure 9).

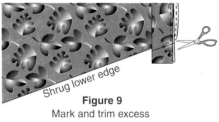

Figure 9
Mark and trim excess
facing ¼" from lower edge.

12. Keeping the underarm edges of the shrug out of the way, stitch the facing ends together and press the seams open. Turn the facing to the inside and press. Pin in place and then stitch close to the inner edge (Figure 10).

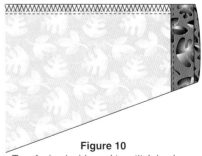

Figure 10
Turn facing inside and topstitch in place.

13. From 2-inch-wide facing strip, cut a neckline facing 17 inches long (the same for all sizes). Fold in half lengthwise and press as you did for the other facing strips. Mark the center of the strip and the center of the back neckline on wthe shrug.

14. With right sides facing and centers matching, pin the facing strip to the back neckline, continuing along the seam line to the ends of the front panels; turn the raw ends inside at each end of the facing. Stitch ¼ inch from the raw edges (Figure 11).

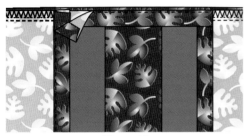

Figure 11
Pin and stitch facing to upper edge of shrug.

15. Turn the facing to the wrong side of the shrug along the neckline and press. Pin in place along the folded edges. Topstitch the neckline facing in place, pivoting across the short ends and meeting up with the previous front facing topstitching lines (Figure 12). ❖

Figure 12
Topstitch neckline facing in place.

Optional Embellishments

• Select and machine-embroider a design of your choice on each front panel. Mirror-image the motifs to achieve a pleasing symmetrical layout.

• Apply paper-backed fusible web to scraps of the main fabric. Cut and fuse geometric shapes, adding fusible bias tape accents if desired. Cover the raw edges of the appliqués with satin stitching.

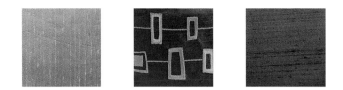

BOLDLY STITCHED

Design by Linda Turner Griepentrog

Embroider lustrous silk dupioni in bright colors for a pretty accessory that is sure to catch a second look when you pair it with coordinating wardrobe brights or basics. Go wild and stitch it boldly in your favorite colors and designs.

Finished Size
9 x 10 x 2½ inches, excluding handles

Technique
Machine embroidery

Materials
• 44/45-inch-wide silk dupioni
    ⅔ yard for outer bag
    ¾ yard for lining, bag overlays and handles
• 1¼ yards 45-inch-wide tailoring-weight fusible interfacing (see Note below)
• 2¼ x 10-inch rectangle heavyweight nonwoven stabilizer (Timtex, for example) for bottom support
• 1¾ yards ¼- or ⅜-inch-diameter cotton cable cord for handles
• All-purpose thread to match fabrics
• Pattern tracing cloth or tissue
• 12-weight cotton embroidery thread
• Bobbin thread for machine embroidery
• Size 90/14 needle for the embroidery
• Tear-away or lightweight cutaway stabilizer
• Embroidery design(s) of your choice, no larger than 5 x 10 inches (Husqvarna Viking Geometric Sensations design #6908 from Disk 69 shown)

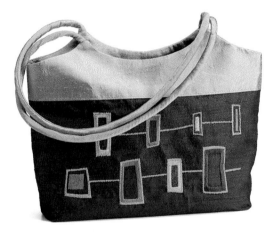

• Tailor's chalk or air-soluble marker
• ½-inch-wide strips paper-backed fusible web
• ½-inch-diameter magnetic snap fastener
• Computerized sewing machine with embroidery unit and mid-size hoop
• Zipper foot
• Basic sewing tools and equipment

Note: *Avoid nonwoven interfacings with the fusible applied in a dot pattern; the dots will strike through and show on the right side of the silk dupioni. Always test your interfacing choice first.*

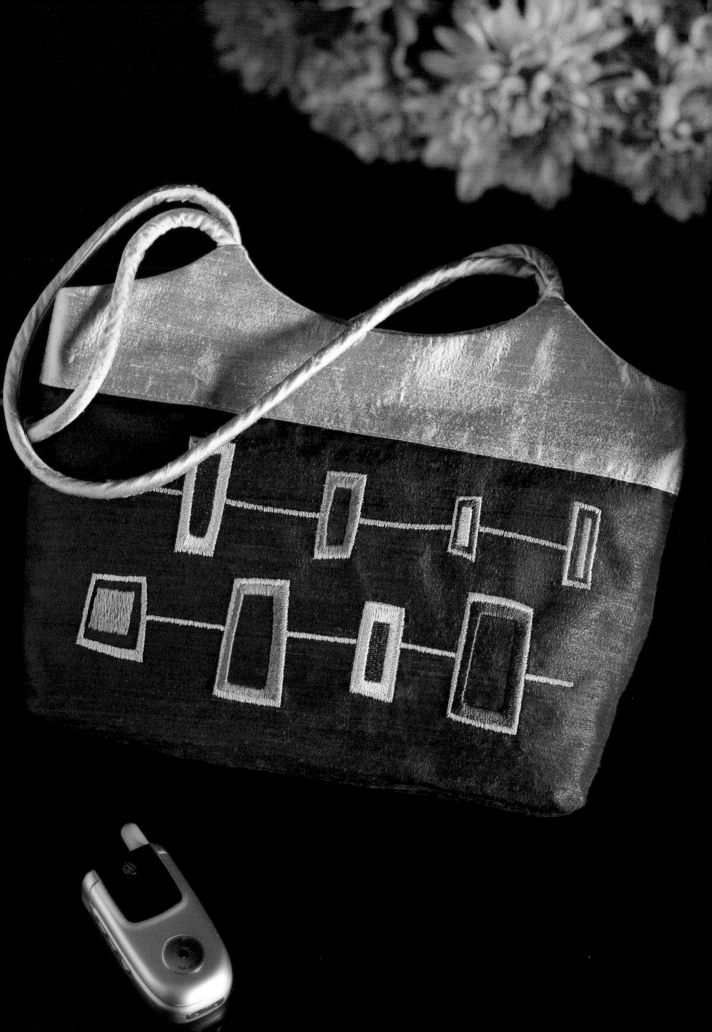

Cutting

• Enlarge the bag pattern (Figure 1) on pattern tracing cloth or tissue and cut out.

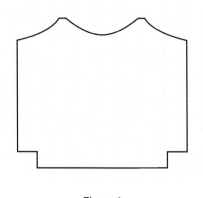

Figure 1
Boldly Stitched Bag Front/Back
1 Square = 1"

• Draw a line 3 inches below the upper edge of the bag at the center to create the pattern for the bag overlay; trace onto another piece of pattern tracing cloth or tissue (Figure 2). Cut out.

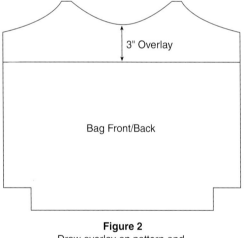

3" Overlay

Bag Front/Back

Figure 2
Draw overlay on pattern and
trace onto pattern tracing paper.

• From the outer bag silk fabric, cut two bag bodies.
• From the silk lining fabric, cut two bag bodies, two overlays and two 1½ x 24-inch bias strips for the handles.
• From the interfacing, cut four bag bodies, two bag overlays and two 1½-inch squares for the snap reinforcement.

• Following the manufacturer's instructions, fuse each interfacing piece to the wrong side of its matching silk piece.

Embroidery

1. Use tailor's chalk or an air-soluble marker to mark the center axis for the embroidery design(s) on the outer bag front where desired.

2. Download the embroidery design to the machine. Insert the size 90/14 needle and thread the machine with 12-weight thread. Before embroidering with this thread, read the tips in Thread Tricks on page 21.

3. Hoop tear-away or lightweight cutaway stabilizer with the bag front, centering the design placement marking with the hoop placement lines. Attach the hoop to the machine and complete the embroidery in the desired colors. Remove the hoop from the machine and trim the stabilizer close to the design. Unhoop the fabric and press from the wrong side.

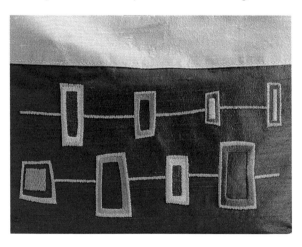

Bag Assembly

Note: Use ¼-inch-wide seams unless otherwise directed.

1. With right sides facing, pin and sew the outer bag side and bottom seams (Figure 3). Do not stitch the corner cutouts. Press the seams open.

Figure 3
Stitch bag pieces together at side and bottom edges.

2. With right sides facing, stitch the overlays together at the side seams. Press the seam allowances open and trim the ends at an angle as shown in Figure 4 to reduce bulk. Machine-baste ⅜ inch from the lower edge of the overlay.

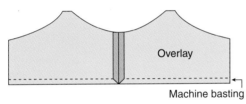

Figure 4
Trim lower ends of seam allowances at an angle.

3. Turn under and press the lower edge of the overlay along the basting. Remove the basting. Slip the overlay over the outer bag, align raw edges and seam line and pin in place. Stitch along the lower turned edge (Figure 5).

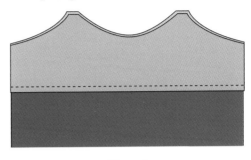

Figure 5
Slip overlay onto bag; stitch.

4. Zigzag close to the upper raw edges, stitching through all layers

5. Fold each corner of the outer bag with side and bottom seam lines aligned and stitch ¼ inch from the raw edges to box the bag bottom (Figure 6 on page 22).

Thread Tricks

The secret to the bold, colorful embroidery on this bag is 12-weight thread. The increased thickness and slight sheen of the cotton thread makes the stitching stand out from the bag surface. For successful embroidery, follow these helpful tips:

• Enlarge the embroidery design to make room for the larger-than-normal thread size. The featured design was increased from its original 82mm x 163mm size to 142mm x 238mm.

• Use a size 90/14 needle to allow the thread to pass through the needle eye without abrasion.

• If possible, slow down the embroidery speed on the machine.

• Disengage the machine's automatic thread-cutting mechanism, because it may not clip the heavier thread close enough.

• Clean the machine bobbin and needle area partway through the project, because the thread tends to build up lint as it stitches.

• Pull uncovered thread ends to the fabric wrong side and secure with tailor's knots.

Figure 6
Align side and bottom seams.
Stitch across corners.

6. On the wrong side of each bag lining piece, fuse a 1½-inch interfacing square in place ¾ inch below the cut edge at the center. Following the manufacturer's directions, install the magnetic snap at the center on the lining right side, positioning it so the center of each half of the snap is 1½ inches below the lining raw edge (Figure 7).

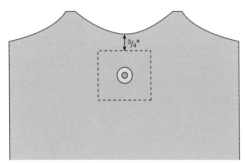

Figure 7
Reinforce lining with interfacing
and apply magnetic snaps.

7. With right sides facing, sew the lining pieces together as for the outer bag, but leave a 4-inch-long opening in the center of the bottom seam. Press the seams open. Box the corners as shown in Figure 6 for the bag. Do not turn the lining right side out.

8. From the cable cord, cut two 28-inch-long pieces. Wrap a 1½ x 24-inch bias strip around each piece, right sides together, beginning at the center of the cord as shown in Figure 8. Attach the zipper foot to the machine. Stitch across the centered end of the cord and then close to the cord. Avoid catching the cord in the stitching.

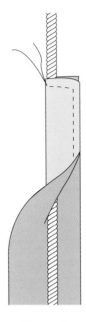

Figure 8
Cover cord with bias.

9. To turn the cord right side out, slide the stitched tube over the excess cord length. Cut across the stitched end and discard the excess cord (Figure 9).

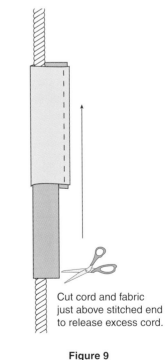

Cut cord and fabric
just above stitched end
to release excess cord.

Figure 9
Slide bias tube back over excess cord.

10. Trim the fabric-covered cords to 22 inches each. With the seam on the handle facing the center of the bag front or back, pin the handle ends to the extensions on the upper edges. Machine-baste in place a scant ¼ inch from the raw edges.

11. With right sides facing and seams aligned, tuck the outer bag into the lining and pin the upper edges together. Stitch ¼ inch from the raw edges, backstitching over each handle end for added security. Turn the bag right side out through the opening in the bottom of the lining. Turn the opening edges in and stitch together close to the turned edge.

12. Tuck the 2¼ x 10-inch piece of heavyweight stabilizer into the bag bottom to test the fit. It should fit easily into the corners and lie flat in the bag bottom without buckling. Trim, if necessary, for a good fit.

13. From lining scraps, cut a 7½ x 10½-inch strip. Center the heavyweight stabilizer on the wrong side of the strip with ¼ inch of the lining panel extending at each short end. Wrap the excess over the stabilizer ends and press (Figure 10).

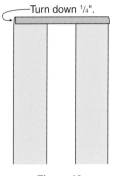

Turn down ¼".

Figure 10
Center stabilizer on lining. Turn under and press excess lining at each short end.

14. Fold the lining over the stabilizer on one side. On the remaining side, turn under and press so the raw edge meets the edge of the stabilizer. Apply a strip of ½-inch-wide fusible web to the lining turn-under allowance close to the pressed edge and remove the backing paper. Turn the lining over onto the lining-covered stabilizer and fuse in place.

15. Tuck the covered rectangle, seam side down, into the bottom of the bag. Use matching thread to catch the short ends of the lining cover to the bag lining to keep the bottom support in place during use. Otherwise, the weight of what you carry in the bag will displace it. ❖

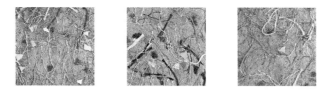

MAKE MINE CONFETTI

Design by Patsy Moreland

Scatter thread and ribbon clippings over the surface of the pieces for a simple vest to create the colorful confetti surface trapped under tulle. Add touches of metallic stitching, assorted trims and beads to make this one-of-a-kind wearable.

Finished Size
Your size

Technique
Thread and fiber confetti

Materials
- Simple vest pattern of your choice in your size (with or without front zipper, as you choose)
- Lightweight cotton denim or similar-weight fabric in the desired color for the vest (see pattern envelope for yardage)
- White or off-white bridal tulle in vest yardage listed on the pattern envelope; test color over the vest fabric. Other colors may work depending on the desired finished effect.
- 9 x 12-inch sheets lightweight paper-backed fusible web—enough to cover the entire surface of the vest front and back pieces
- 3 yards ¼-inch-wide satin ribbon in colors to match the rayon embroidery flosses
- 2 skeins each of rayon embroidery floss in each of 6 or 7 colors of your choice
- Metallic embroidery floss in gold and silver or other colors of your choice
- All-purpose sewing thread to match vest fabric
- *Optional:* assorted colors sewing thread
- Assorted embellishments:
    Fusible crystals
    Beads and buttons in colors to match thread and ribbon
    Charms
    Assorted silk flowers
    Trim of your choice for neckline edges (measure pattern pieces to determine required yardage)
- *Optional:* separating zipper and coordinating zipper pull
- Teflon press cloth or parchment paper
- 2 (1-quart-size) self-sealing plastic bags
- Steam iron
- Basic sewing tools and equipment

Cutting

• Preshrink the vest fabric and press to remove all wrinkles.

• Cut the vest pieces from the denim following the pattern layout.

• Cut the floss and threads into assorted lengths ranging from 1½–4 inches long and place in a self-sealing plastic bag (Photo 1).

Photo 1

• Angle-cut the ribbons as shown in Photo 2.

Photo 2

• Cut oversize rectangles of tulle for the vest fronts and back.

Assembly

1. Place the vest back face up on a large, heat-resistant surface.

2. Referring to the manufacturer's directions, cover the vest back with sheets of the fusible web, butting the sheets edge to edge. Trim excess web even with the vest back raw edges (Photo 3).

Photo 3

3. Sprinkle cut threads and ribbons onto the web (Photo 4).

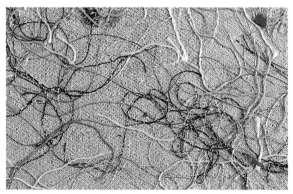

Photo 4

4. Place the rectangle of tulle over the threads on the vest back, taking care not to disturb the confetti (Photo 5).

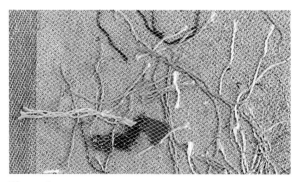

Photo 5

5. Place the press cloth or a sheet of parchment paper on top of the tulle. Preheat steam iron to the setting for cotton (steam).

6. Fuse the tulle and confetti to the denim in small sections, leaving the iron in place for 10–15 seconds. Do not slide iron; use a lifting/placing motion instead, overlapping the just-fused area slightly as you replace the iron on an unfused area.

7. Trim excess tulle even with the denim edges.

8. Add confetti to the vest front pieces in the same manner.

9. Assemble the vest following the directions in the pattern guidesheet.

10. Position trim around the vest neckline and stitch in place. Add buttons and fusible-crystal embellishments as desired (Photo 6).

Photo 6

11. Arrange the desired embellishments on the vest fronts and backs as desired and hand-sew in place.

12. If your vest has a zipper, attach a coordinating zipper pull. ❖

PAINT 'N' FUSE

Design by Lynn Weglarz

Be your own fabric designer using this unique technique. Paint on fusible web and then cut and fuse pieces of it to fabric to create the colorful trim for this swingy jacket. It's also great for embellishing a handbag or tote, home decor projects or art quilts.

Finished Size
Your size

Technique
Painted fusible web

Materials
• Jacket pattern of your choice
• Solid-colored fabric with smooth or lightly textured surface (not a print) for the jacket in yardage listed on pattern envelope
• Interfacing and notions as listed on the pattern envelope
• *Optional:* ⅓ yard lightweight coordinating fabric for Hong Kong finish on jacket seams
• ¼–½ yard tulle or other sheer fabric for overlays on painted fusible (see Project Notes on page 31 before purchasing)
• 1–2 yards lightweight paper-backed fusible web (see Note at right); you may need extra for experimenting with the painting technique

• Teflon press sheet
• Acrylic paints for fabric
• Decorative threads to match either paints, tulle or jacket fabric
• *Optional:* dress form
• Disposable foam paintbrushes (1-inch-wide for broad strokes, smaller widths for more detailed motifs)
• Disposable paper cups, paper plates and paper towels
• Low-tack tape (blue painter's tape from the hardware store)
• Rotary cutter, mat and ruler
• Waterproof work surface, such as an old rotary-cutting mat
• Basic sewing tools and equipment

Note: *You must be able to stitch through the lightweight fusible web, so choose one that will not gum up the needle. Buy extra fusible web if you want to do extensive experimentation with the painting technique.*

Painting on Fusible Web

• It is easier to paint the strips working from the top to the bottom along the length of the strip.

• Use one paintbrush for each color, or clean the brush thoroughly after each color use.

• Add paint colors one at a time with drying time in between. When you touch the painted area, none should come off on your fingers if it is completely dry.

• For a watercolor effect, add paints, one on top of the other, without drying time.

• Use a dry brush rather than wet for a thicker application of paint, or try squeezing paint directly from the tube onto the fusible web. Play with the paint. As the "designer," you get to choose what you want to do to create the desired finished results. Playing with paints can become addictive.

• Try not to repaint an area too much, because the motion will start to peel the fusible web away—but you might like the resulting look.

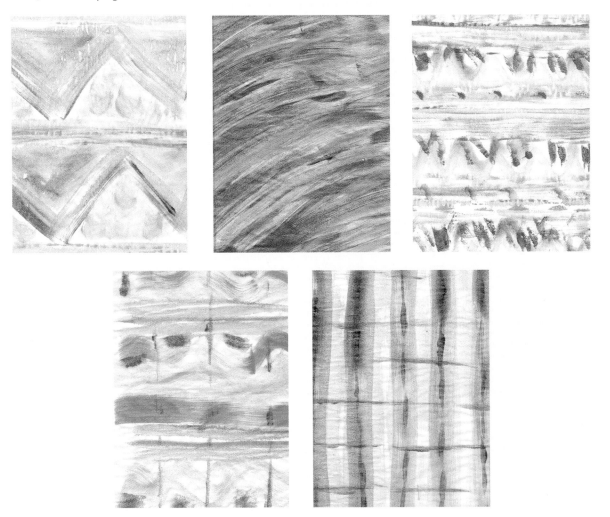

Painting the Fusible Web

Project Notes: *After the painted fusible web is applied to the surface of your project, a layer of sheer bridal tulle or lightweight sheer fabric is adhered to the design and trimmed close to the edges. The sheerness and color of the tulle will affect the finished look. The differences can be dramatic or subtle, so it would be best to purchase small amounts of the colors you want to test, or wait until you have applied the fusible to the background fabric and then take it to the fabric store to test your choices and watch how your fabric design changes.*

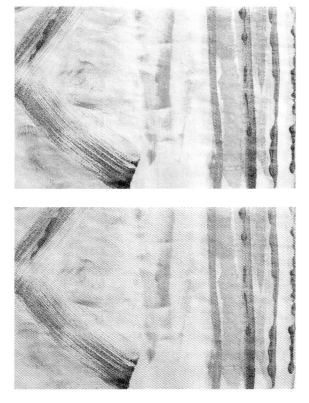

1. If the fusible web you are using has protective transfer paper on both sides, remove it from one side, leaving the fusible web attached to one piece of paper.

Note: *If the web you are using has no protective paper, you can still paint on it, but you may need to anchor it to the work surface with more tape and use your free hand to keep it down while you paint.*

2. Tape the paper with web to the work surface, fusible side up. Don't be concerned if bits of the fusible web peel away in places—this will simply make the painted fusible web more interesting.

3. Squeeze fabric paints onto the paper plate in small amounts.

4. Fill a few paper cups halfway with water. Dip a paintbrush into water and squeeze out excess water, leaving the foam slightly damp.

5. Read through Painting on Fusible Web for helpful tips before you begin painting the web. Then throw caution to the wind and begin to paint the design of your choice. It can be random or planned, striped, plaid, floral, geometric—you are the designer! If you need inspiration, work from a photo, a magazine clipping or an actual piece of fabric that has colors and designs you like. Anyone can do this type of free-form work!

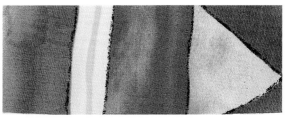

6. Allow the painted web to dry thoroughly, at least 24 hours, before you use it to embellish your project.

Jacket Assembly & Embellishment

Project Note: Directions below are customized to the Getting to the Point jacket shown in the photos. Refer to the design placement process outlined in the steps below as needed for the jacket pattern you have chosen.

1. Cut the jacket pieces from the jacket fabric following the pattern layout. Sew the jacket fronts to the backs and complete any other necessary construction as directed in the guidesheet up to sewing the side seams. Do not add facings, sleeves or collar yet. Prepare the inner pockets but do not attach them. Machine-baste along the seam lines at the front and side seam edges as a helpful guideline for design placement.

2. Serge-finish the seam edges on each piece of the jacket or see Hong Kong Finish on the next page for a lovely bound-edge finish for unlined jackets. If you are using the Getting to the Point jacket pattern, finish the hem edges following the guidesheet and using the same finish you chose for the seam edges.

3. Cut painted fusible web into desired shapes, sizes and widths. Eliminate painted areas you don't like by cutting around them and discarding them.

4. With wrong sides together, pin the jacket side seams along the side seam lines and place the jacket on a dress form, if available. Otherwise, place the jacket on a hanger on an over-the-door hook so you can plan the painted web placement. Pin strips or shapes in place, painted side out. For design continuity, be sure to use the web on the jacket back as well. Continuing strips across the shoulder seam and onto the back is a good way (but not the only way) to do this. Pin the pieces in the desired locations.

5. If you are using the Getting to the Point jacket as shown, pin the front and back neckband to the jacket as if sewn in place. If necessary, adjust the placement of the strips on the jacket front and back for better placement in relation to the band. Do not plan design placement on the band yet.

6. When you are happy with the arrangement of the painted pieces on the jacket front and back, unpin the front band and side seams. At the ironing board, unpin the painted fusible strips one at a time, turn over so the paper side is facing up, and reposition on the jacket. Cover the strip to be fused with a Teflon press sheet and fuse the strip or piece in place from the paper side following the manufacturer's directions. Repeat to fuse the remaining pieces in place, one by one. Allow the strips to cool completely and then carefully remove the backing paper from each piece.

7. Cut oversize strips or squares of the tulle or sheer fabric and position over the painted strips. Place the Teflon press sheet on top and fuse the fabric to the fused painted strips. Allow to cool and then trim the tulle or sheer fabric close to the outer edges of the painted-and-fused strips.

Note: Until the tulle is fused into place, the fusible web will pick up lint. If you touch an iron to it directly, the fusible will stick to the bottom of the iron.

8. Using decorative thread, randomly stitch through the tulle and painted fusible for added decorative dimension.

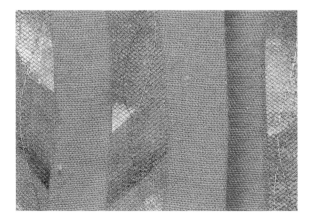

9. Following the pattern guidesheet, complete the jacket up to the front band (don't set in sleeves yet).

10. Drape the jacket over a dress form or place on a hanger and pin the jacket band in place again. Position and pin strips of the painted web on the band as desired. If the painted web goes around the back band (neckline), make sure to position it so that it lies on the outer portion of the band, not the part that will lie against the back of your neck in the finished garment. When satisfied with the web placement, unpin the band, take it to the ironing board and apply the strips, tulle and stitching as directed for the jacket front and back.

11. Following the pattern guidesheet, complete the jacket construction up to the sleeves. Machine-baste the underarm seam in the sleeves and baste the sleeves into the jacket armholes to check the fit. Decide if you want to add painted web to the sleeve-cap area of the sleeves. Position web as desired and pin in place. Remove the sleeves from the armholes, undo the basting in the underarm seams and apply the painted web, tulle and stitching as you did for other sections of the jacket.

12. Permanently stitch the underarm seams, press open and finish the seam edges.

13. Interface the cuffs and assemble as directed in the guidesheet. Pin the cuffs to the sleeves and turn up where indicated. Decide where to position the painted web if desired. Make sure it is on the side of the cuff that will be turned to the outside of the jacket sleeve. Unpin the cuffs and fuse the web in place as desired.

14. Attach the cuffs, finish the seam edges and turn them up onto the sleeves. Set the sleeve into the jacket and finish the seam edges.

15. If you have used a pattern other than Getting to the Point, hem the jacket, finishing the raw edges with serging or the Hong Kong finish as desired. ❖

Hong Kong Finish

1. Cut 2-inch-wide strips across the width of the lightweight coordinating fabric you've chosen for the seam finish.

Note: *The jacket shown has no curved edges to finish with Hong Kong binding so straight-grain strips are easy to use. For curved edges, cut bias strips instead. You may need more fabric for this cutting method.*

2. Sew the strips together with bias seams (Figure 1) to make one long piece. Trim the seams to ¼ inch wide and press open.

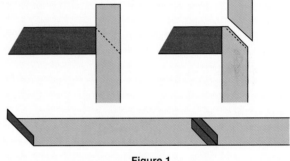

Figure 1
Sew strips together with bias seams.

3. Fold the strip in half lengthwise with wrong sides facing and press.

4. Refer to Figure 2 for steps 4 and 5. To finish the seam edge, align the raw edges of the strip with the seam-allowance raw edge. Stitch ¼ inch from the edges, using a ¼-inch presser foot for accurate seaming (Figure 2a).

5. Press the binding toward the raw edges and wrap to the underside. Press and pin in place. From the right side of the seam allowance, stitch in the ditch of the seam to catch the underlayer of the binding (Figure 2b).

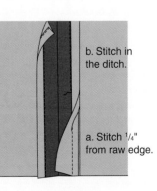

b. Stitch in the ditch.

a. Stitch ¼" from raw edge.

Figure 2
Hong Kong Finish

PUT IT IN YOUR PIPING

Design by Linda Turner Griepentrog

Who said piping has to be ordinary? Use the decorative stitches on your machine to jazz up this traditional trim for one-of-a-kind accents on garments, handbags or home decor accessories like this sampler pillow.

Finished Size
18 inches square

Technique
Decorative piping variations

Materials
- 1 yard 60-inch-wide medium-weight black cotton fabric
- ⅛ yard 45-inch-wide red cotton fabric
- ¼ yard 60-inch-wide black-and-white striped cotton fabric for piping around outer edge
- 7 (1–1½-inch-wide) strips coordinating cotton prints for the pieced piping (four different prints used for this pillow)
- Assorted narrow trims, ribbons and braids for the tied piping
- 1 yard ¼-inch-wide beaded ribbon for the beaded piping
- 2¼ yards ¹²⁄₃₂-inch-diameter cotton cord for the novelty piping
- 2¼ yards 1-inch-diameter cotton cord for the outer-edge piping
- 12-weight cotton embroidery thread
- ¼-inch-wide paper-backed fusible web
- 18-inch-square pillow form
- Removable marker or chalk
- *Optional:* 1 (2¾-inch-long) bone bead or other decorative bead or button accent
- All-purpose thread to match pillow fabric and contrasting for bobbin
- Size 90/14 needle
- Masking tape
- Zipper foot
- Fabric/craft glue
- *Optional:* Liquid seam sealant
- Rotary cutter, mat and ruler
- Sewing machine with embroidery stitches
- Basic sewing tools and equipment

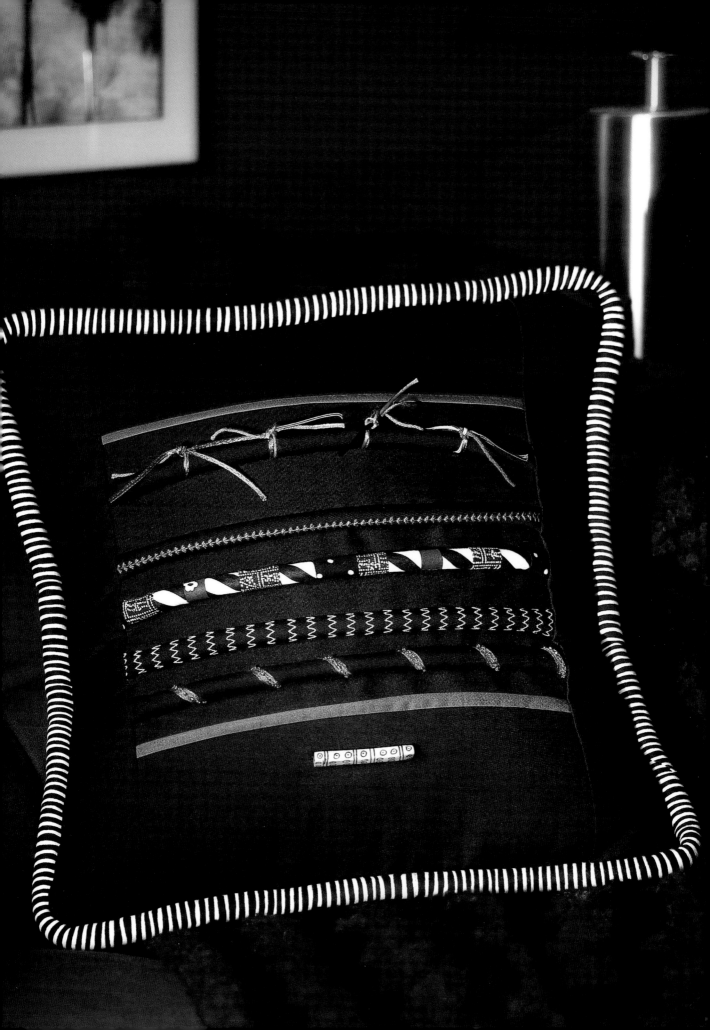

Cutting

• From the black fabric, cut two 12 x 19-inch rectangles for the pillow back. For the piped-and-pieced pillow front panel, cut six 2½ x 14-inch strips. Cut five 2½ x 14-inch strips for the piping. For the top and bottom borders on the piped panel, cut two 6 x 14-inch strips. For the side borders, cut two 3½ x 19-inch strips.

• From the red fabric, cut one 1¾ x 30-inch strip for the flat piping.

• From the striped fabric for the outer-edge piping, cut two 3-inch-wide strips across the fabric grain.

Assembly

Note: *Use ½-inch-wide seam allowances unless otherwise directed.*

1. Make a narrow double hem on one long edge of each rectangle for the pillow back. Overlap the hemmed edges to form a 19-inch square and baste the edges together (Figure 1).

Figure 1
Lap back panels to create
a 19" square; baste.

2. Embellish the five 2½ x 14-inch strips of black fabric for the piping following the directions in Novelty Piping How-Tos on page 38.

3. To complete the piping pieces, cut five 16-inch-long pieces of cotton cord. Before cutting, wrap the cord with masking tape at each location and cut through the center of the tape. Never cut cotton cord without taping the ends or it will untwist, making it unusable.

4. Attach the zipper foot and adjust so the needle is positioned to the left of the foot. Machine-baste as close to the cord as possible (Figure 2). Trim the seam allowances to an even ½ inch along the length of each completed piping.

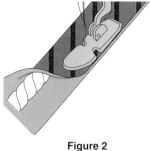

Figure 2
Wrap bias around cord and stitch.

5. Put contrasting thread on the bobbin. Pin and machine-baste a piece of piping to the right side of one edge of five of the 2½ x 14-inch black strips. Arrange the piped strips in the desired order with the remaining black strip at the bottom. Pin and sew the strips together, stitching from the side with the contrasting basting. Stitch just inside the basting. It will feel like you are crowding the cord in the piping (Figure 3).

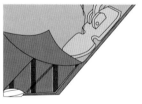

Figure 3
Sew the piping panels together,
stitching close to the cord.

6. Fold the red fabric strip in half lengthwise with wrong sides together to create flat piping strips; press. Cut two 14-inch-long pieces from the strip and stitch the strips to the top and bottom edges of the piping sampler. Trim the excess even with the sampler edges. Add a 6 x 14-inch strip to each end of the sampler and trim the excess even with the sampler edges (Figure 4). Press the seams toward the outer strips with the flat piping turned toward the piping sampler.

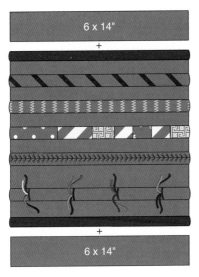

Figure 4
Arrange piped strips, borders
and flat piping; sew together.

7. Trim the piped panel to 13 x 19 inches. Zigzag across both short edges of the piping sampler to flatten the piping ends (Figure 5).

Figure 5
Zigzag over ends of piping to flatten.

8. Pin and stitch a 3½ x 19-inch black strip to each long edge of the piping panel to complete the pillow top. Press the seams toward the border strips.

9. For the outer-edge piping, sew the two strips of black-and-white striped fabric together to make one long piece. Use a ¼-inch-wide seam allowance and press the seam open. Cover the remaining cotton cord with the fabric strip to make piping as shown in Figure 2 on page 36.

Piping Possibilities

Let your imagination run wild to create decorative piping of your own design and in different color palettes.

• If you have an embroidery machine, use it to add color and texture to the fabric strips for your piping. Remember that the area that's actually seen on the finished piping is relatively small (unless the piping is quite large), so "audition" designs by looking at only a small portion to see how they look. Small or repetitive motifs and allover motifs show up best. Depending on the embroidery motif, it's sometimes better to embroider an entire rectangle of fabric with an allover pattern, and then cut the piping strips from the embellished fabric.

• Try stitching with variegated threads to add pizzazz to piping designs.

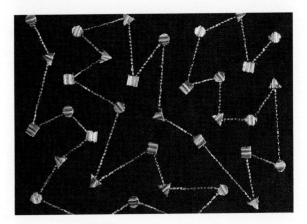

10. Beginning in the center of one edge of the pillow top, position and baste the piping to the outer edge. Clip the piping seam allowance at each corner for a smooth turn (Figure 6).

Clip piping seam allowance at corners.

Figure 6
Baste piping to outer edge.

11. When you reach the beginning of the piping, clip the cotton cord ends so they butt together as shown in Figure 7. Turn under the fabric as shown to cover the ends and complete the basting.

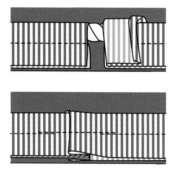

Figure 7
Join piping ends.

12. With right sides facing and the pillow front on top, pin the pillow front and back pieces together. Stitch close to the cord using a zipper foot and crowding the cord for a smooth, tight fit. Stitch just inside the previous basting. Turn the pillow cover right side out through the opening in the pillow back.

13. Create either a knot or a bow on the tied piping sample and use fabric/craft glue to anchor the knot in place to prevent slick trims from coming untied. Trim the ends to the desired length and apply seam sealant to the cord ends to prevent raveling, if needed.

14. Sew the bone bead to the pillow front, if desired. Insert the pillow form through the back opening. ❖

Novelty Piping How-Tos

Vertical Decorative Stitch

1. Insert the size 90/14 needle in the machine and thread the machine with 12-weight thread in a contrasting color.

2. Choose a decorative machine stitch and test-stitch it on a fabric scrap; adjust the length and tensions as needed.

3. Chalk-mark a stitching line on the right side through the center of one of the 2½ x 14-inch black piping strips. Stitch along the line with the decorative stitch (Figure 1).

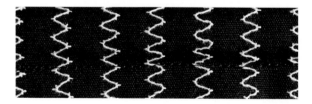

Figure 1
Stitch along line in center of strip.

Horizontal Decorative Stitch

1. Complete steps 1 and 2 as directed above for Vertical Decorative Stitch.

2. Using the selected decorative stitch, do parallel rows of stitching on a 2¼ x 14-inch black fabric strip (Figure 2). Begin and end stitching at the long edges of the strip and use the outer edge of the presser foot as the guide for spacing them an even distance apart. For other spacing, mark the desired stitching lines on the strip or attach an adjustable seam guide to the presser foot and secure it the desired distance from the needle.

Figure 2
Stitch parallel rows across piping strip.

Pieced Piping

1. Stitch the coordinating print strips together in the desired order using ¼-inch-wide seam allowances. The resulting strip unit should measure 7–8 inches wide x 10 inches long.

2. Press all seams in one direction in the resulting strip-pieced unit.

3. Using rotary-cutting tools, cut two 2½-inch-wide segments from the strip unit (Figure 3).

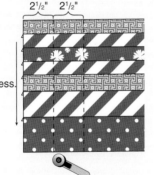

Figure 3
Sew print strips together.
Cut 2½"-wide segments.

4. Using ¼-inch-wide seam allowances, sew the two segments together, end to end, to make one long pieced strip for the piping. If it is not at least 14 inches long, cut an additional segment from the remainder of the strip unit and add it to the strip.

Beaded Piping

1. Back the beaded ribbon with paper-backed fusible web and apply it diagonally to the piping strip, spacing the pieces approximately 1¾ inches apart.

2. Use the tip of the iron (or a small craft iron) to fuse the trim in place.

Note: *If the trim has plastic beads, heat may damage them, so use fabric glue to hold the strips in place instead. Test first.*

3. Once the trim is secure, remove any beads from the seam allowances to avoid damaging the needle as you assemble and apply the piping.

Tied Piping

1. Cut the assorted trims into 6-inch lengths.

2. Using a removable marker or chalk, draw lines across a 2½ x 14-inch black strip at 2-inch intervals.

3. Stitch groups of two trims at each edge marking ¼ inch from the piping-strip edge. To keep the trims out of the way while completing the piping, tie the opposing pairs together (Figure 4).

Figure 4
Sew strips at marks and tie together in pairs.

FOILED AGAIN!

Design by Lucy B. Gray

With simple materials and this easy technique, you can create gorgeous art cloth to use for a pretty scarf, a small handbag or an art-to-wear jacket. Use your iron to burnish colorful foil motifs onto mini "art cloths" for this party scarf, or incorporate foiled fabrics into other artful sewing projects of your own design.

Finished Size
6½ x 60 inches, excluding fringe

Technique
Foiling on fabric

Materials
- 44/45-inch-wide silk or rayon dressmaker fabrics
    - ⅓ yard large dramatic print (abstract or figural design)
    - ⅓ yard small repeating print in colors that set off the large print (stripes, polka dots, checks)
    - ⅓ yard solid in a color that contrasts with large print
    - ⅓ yard solid in a color that blends with large print
- 6½ x 62-inch piece low-loft polyester batting
- Lightweight fusible interfacing (see Project Note on page 42)
- *Optional:* Lite Steam-A-Seam2 fusible web (see Fearless Foiling on page 44)
- ½ yard 1-inch-wide fringe trim
- *Optional:* pearl cotton thread in same color as either solid fabric for stitched accents
- All-purpose thread to match fabrics
- Liquid seam sealant
- Spray craft adhesive
- *Optional:* spray fabric protector
- Sticky notes
- Foil adhesive
- Metallic foil sheets in several colors
- Low-tack tape
- Stamps, stencils and old toothbrushes
- Newspaper
- Old towel
- Rotary cutter, mat and ruler
- Iron and square of muslin for press cloth
- Basic sewing tools and equipment

Cutting

Project Note: *If one or more of your fabrics is lightweight, apply a layer of lightweight fusible knit or weft-insertion interfacing to the wrong side before cutting. All four of the scarf fabrics should be of similar weight.*

• From each of the four different fabrics, cut four 7 x 12-inch rectangles (with the 12-inch sides along the lengthwise grain) for a total of 16 pieces.
• Cut each of the (16) 7 x 12-inch rectangles into 7-inch-long strips of assorted widths from as narrow as 1½ inches to as wide as 12 inches.

Assembly

1. Arrange the fabric pieces in random order to create two strips that are each 7 inches wide and about 64–66 inches long before seaming them together. Work on a design wall or on the floor so that you can view the arrangements from a distance. Rearrange as desired for the best overall visual effect. The two arrangements need not be identical.

2. Decide which fabric pieces you will foil and mark them with a pin. Keep in mind how the fabric arrangement will look when the scarf is wrapped around your neck (and possibly looped in front). Designs that appear vertical on the floor may change their orientation when the scarf is worn. Also think about the foiling effects you want at the scarf ends, because these will be most visible when the scarf is being worn.

3. Collect the fabrics into two piles as you have arranged them and move to your work surface. Working with one pile at a time, arrange them in order to one side, and then pull out the ones marked for foiling.

Note: *The next two steps require experimentation on scraps first in order to get a feel for the right amount of adhesive, heat and burnishing. Practice before foiling on the scarf pieces.*

4. Apply the foil adhesive to the fabric in a light, even layer (see Fearless Foiling, page 44, for application ideas). Allow adhesive to dry for two hours.

5. Place an old towel on your ironing board to pad it. Set your iron on "cotton" with no steam. Place the foil sheet, colored side up, over the fabric, and use the tip and side of your iron to burnish the foil into the areas where you applied the adhesive. Wait until the foil has cooled, and then gently peel it away from the fabric. If the foil isn't transferring, you may have applied too little adhesive, or the foil is wrong side up, or you aren't burnishing with sufficient heat or pressure. If you have applied too little adhesive, simply reapply more with a small paintbrush over the previous spots and wait two more hours before refoiling. (Photo 1).

Photo 1

6. After you have foiled the pieces as desired, arrange all fabrics in the two original rows in the order previously determined. Of course, you may rearrange the pieces, if desired, so that the foiled pieces will be most visible in the finished scarf panels. When you are pleased with the arrangements, number the pieces with sticky notes to help keep them in order for sewing.

7. Using ¼-inch-wide seam allowances, sew the pieces together for each scarf panel. Press the seams open, using a press cloth to protect the fabrics and foiled areas from the iron (and vice versa). The finished panels should measure 60½ inches long. Trim any uneven edges using rotary-cutting tools so both panels are the same size.

8. Working outside (or in an unused room or area in your home or garage), place one scarf panel wrong side up on top of a piece of newspaper. Lightly spray the fabric surface with craft adhesive. Carry the length back to your worktable and lay the batting on the sprayed side. With your hand, pat the batting to bond it lightly to the scarf. Use a light hand because the fabrics may dimple on the right side if too firmly bonded to the batting. Turn the panel over and make sure the seams are all lying parallel to each other and perpendicular to the side edges (slippery fabrics can wiggle off grain). Trim ¼ inch from the outer edges of the batting to eliminate bulky seams (Figure 1).

Figure 1
Trim batting to expose ¼" of
the scarf panel all around.

9. Cut two 6½-inch-long pieces of the fringe trim and dab a little liquid seam sealant on the cut ends of the fringe headings; allow to dry thoroughly. Align the fringe headings on the right side of the batting-backed scarf panel and pin in place. To keep the fringe ends in place so they won't get caught in the seams, tape them to the scarf panel temporarily (Figure 2).

Figure 2
Tape fringe ends in place.

10. With right sides facing, pin the remaining scarf panel to the one with the fringe, leaving a 4-inch-long unpinned section in the center of one long side. With the batting side face up, stitch the layers together ¼ inch from the raw edges, right next to the batting edges, leaving the unpinned area unstitched to allow for turning (Figure 3).

Figure 3
Stitch next to batting.

11. Turn the scarf right side out through the opening and remove the tape on the fringe ends before tugging gently on the ends to turn the ends and corners completely. Press the outer edges of the scarf, using a press cloth as needed to protect the fabric. Turn under and finger-press the opening edges and slipstitch them together.

12. Using pearl cotton, add a decorative running stitch on selected panels (Photo 2), but stitch only through one scarf layer and into the batting, without catching the scarf layer on the other side. Sewing through all layers will lessen the drape of the finished scarf.

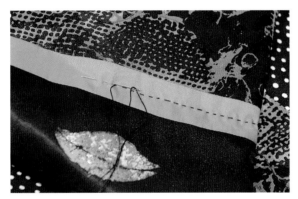

Photo 2

13. *Optional:* *Apply a light coat of fabric protector to one side of the scarf and allow to dry. Add a second coat and allow to dry. Repeat on the remaining side of the scarf. This helps delay body oils from soiling the scarf if you wear it with collarless tops.*

14. To care for the finished scarf, hand-wash with mild detergent in cool water and rinse thoroughly. Wrap inside a thick towel and hand-press (don't wring) to squeeze out excess water. Lay the scarf flat to air dry. Do not put it in the dryer—the foil will come off! When the scarf is dry, steam-press it as needed, using a press cloth to protect the fabric and the foiling. ❖

Fearless Foiling

You can create both defined shapes and abstract patterns with foiling—it depends on what you use to apply the adhesive to the fabric. For example, metallic glints were stamped onto an appliquéd design (Photo 1), and defined shapes were stenciled to a piece of art cloth (Photo 2). Virtually anything can be used as an applicator—old toothbrushes, sponges, even parts from plastic fruit containers!

Photo 1   Photo 2

Here are two ways to foil recognizable shapes with clear, definite outlines.

Method One

With this method, the foil is applied evenly, although a faint texture from the web will be visible beneath the foil surface.

1. Cut a shape from Lite Steam-A-Seam 2 fusible web.

2. Heat the fabric with a hot iron, and then peel off the first paper layer and press the shape firmly onto your fabric with the fusible side down.

3. Peel the second paper off. Place the foil, color side up, on the adhesive and burnish with the iron. Peel the foil away when it has cooled, and the shape should have a clear outline like the leaf on the left in Photo 3.

Photo 3

Method Two

In contrast, if you stencil foil adhesive onto the fabric with an old toothbrush, and then apply the foil, the resulting shape will have an irregular stippled appearance like the leaf on the right in Photo 3 above.

Foiled random patterns can accent the design on the fabric. A toothbrush or sponge dipped in adhesive and dabbed here and there on the fabric surface adds an interesting, uneven texture to the overall design when the foil is added (Photo 4).

Photo 4

You can make a complete foiling kit from a plastic fruit container!

1. Cut the smooth section of the lid free and make a stencil from it (such as the leaf shape shown in Photo 3 above).

2. Cut up the rest of the container and use the indented and rippled sections for stamps (Photo 5).

Photo 5

3. Use the bottom divider as a handle for four different stamps created by gluing on bits of sheet foam (Photo 6a and 6b).

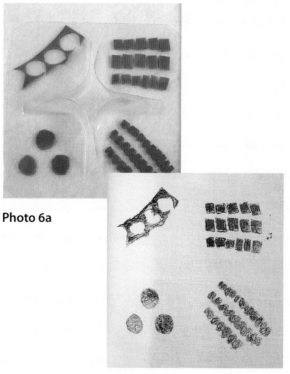

Photo 6a

Photo 6b

BEAD TOSS

Design by Stephanie Corina Goddard

Softly draped and sumptuously dramatic, an elegant evening shawl is trimmed with beaded fringe. Wear it sari-style with the seam at your right shoulder and the front tossed over your left.

Finished Size
104 inches long

Technique
Hand-beaded fringe

Materials
Project Note: *Half of the shawl is a single layer of fabric, so choose a lightweight printed fabric with good color saturation on the wrong side.*

• 2 yards 54–60-inch-wide fabric or 3 yards 44-inch-wide fabric

• Strong hand-sewing thread (button/carpet) to match fabric
• 2-inch-long hand-sewing needle
• Fabric marking pencil
• Beads
  198 size #6 beads
  231 size #8 beads
  99 novelty beads, approximately ¼-inch in diameter
• *Optional:* seam roll
• Basic sewing tools and equipment

Assembly

1. Cut two 36 x 54-inch rectangles from the fabric.

2. Turn under and press a double ¼-inch-wide hem on both long edges of one rectangle only. Stitch close to the inner edge of each hem allowance. Repeat at one short end of the rectangle. Set this piece aside for pleating.

3. Fold the remaining rectangle in half lengthwise with right sides facing and raw edges aligned. Pin and then stitch ½ inch from one short end and the long edges. Trim the corners on the diagonal to eliminate bulk. Slip the tube over the end of the ironing board or tuck a seam roll inside and press the seam allowances open as much as possible before turning it right side out. This will make it easier to turn and press really flat edges at the seams. Turn right side out and press the tube flat.

4. Place each rectangle face up and trim the unfinished short end at an angle as shown in Figure 1.

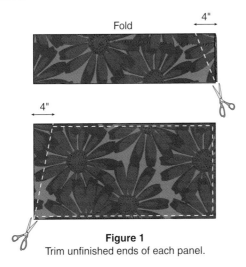

Figure 1
Trim unfinished ends of each panel.

5. Measure 10 inches from the straight end at the bottom edge of the single-layer panel, and then make three deep soft pleats so that it matches the width of the tube. The folded edges of the pleats should point toward the upper edge of the panel. Hand- or machine-baste a scant ½ inch from the raw edges to secure the pleats (Figure 2).

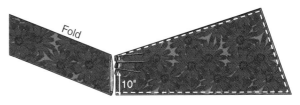

Figure 2
Using tube width as guide, form pleats in single-layer panel. Baste a scant ½" from raw edges.

6. With right sides facing, pin the pleated panel to one layer of the tube. Stitch ½ inch from the raw edges, taking care not to catch the remaining layer of the tube in the stitching (Figure 3). To stabilize the bias grain of the seam line, stitch a second time, ⅛ inch from the first stitching in the seam allowance.

Figure 3
Stitch one layer of tube to pleated edge of remaining panel.

7. Turn under ½ inch at the remaining raw edge and press. Pin in place along the stitching line and slipstitch in place by hand.

8. Use the fabric marking pencil to mark beaded-fringe attachment points at each finished end of the shawl. At the narrower end, evenly space 11 marks; at the wider end, evenly space 22 marks.

9. Make 33 strands of bead fringe. For each strand, thread a single 16-inch-long strand of strong hand-sewing thread onto a 2-inch-long needle. Pick up the beads in the order shown in Figure 4. After adding the last three small beads, insert the needle back through the bead column. Remove the needle, leaving long thread tails.

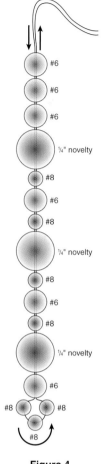

#6
#6
#6
¼" novelty
#8
#6
#8
¼" novelty
#8
#6
#8
¼" novelty
#6
#8   #8
#8

Figure 4
Beading Pattern for Fringe

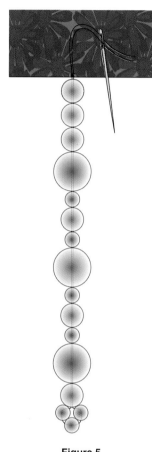

Figure 5
Attaching Bead Fringe.

10. Pull the thread ends even and then pass them together through the needle eye. Take several small stitches at the edge of the fabric, snugging the bead column close to the fabric (Figure 5). Avoid overtightening, which causes the bead column to lose flexibility.

11. Tie a single overhand knot about ⅛ inch from the fabric surface, and then bury the needle between the layers, exiting at least 1 inch away. Tug the threads just enough to cause the knot to pop below the surface; then trim the thread close to the fabric. Repeat to attach the remaining bead columns to the scarf ends at the marked locations. ❖

STAMPED & "HOLE-Y"

Design by Carol Zentgraf

Add your own decorative touches to a wearable art jacket by embellishing it with stamped designs. Eyelets add a little "punch" to the stamped design and echo the jacket's grommet closure.

Finished Size
Your size

Techniques
Grommets
Stamping on fabric

Materials
• Jacket pattern of your choice with peplum (Eyelet Appeal Jacket #IJ727 from Indygo Junction shown; see Note in cutting directions to adapt other patterns for peplum)
• Linen or linenlike fabrics in coordinating colors of your choice for the jacket, peplum and trim as given in the pattern
• 1¼ yards narrow cord for front-closure loops
• Interfacing and notions listed on the pattern envelope
• *Optional:* seam binding
• 5 (⅜-inch-diameter) grommets
• 5 (¾-inch-diameter) decorative buttons
• Grommet pliers
• 14 (⅛-inch-diameter) colored eyelets
• Eyelet pliers
• Clear stamp (floral design) for fabric
• Textile paint
• Textile paint stamp pad

• *Optional:* cellophane or masking tape
• Air- or water-soluble fabric marking pen
• All-purpose thread to match fabrics
• Spoon
• Iron
• Basic sewing tools and equipment

Cutting
• Adjust the pattern to fit as needed.
Note: *If your pattern doesn't have a peplum, you can add one by cutting the jacket front pattern apart at the desired location for the peplum and adding seam allowances to the pattern tissue at the two cut edges (Figure 1).*

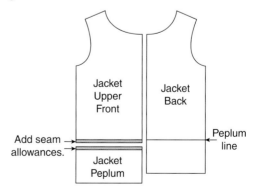

Figure 1
Draw peplum line at desired location.
Cut apart and add seam allowances to cut edges.

- Follow the pattern guidesheet to cut the jacket pieces from the appropriate fabrics.
- From the cord, cut five 8-inch lengths. Tape the ends to prevent raveling.

Assembly

1. Follow the pattern guidesheet to assemble the jacket and press.

2. Finish the seam-allowance edges with serging or binding.

3. Evenly space markings for five grommets on the right front placket for the grommet closure, placing them ¼ inch from the finished edge. Use a fabric marking pen to draw around the inside of each grommet to mark the placement (Figure 2).

Figure 2
Space and mark grommet placements
with outer edge of grommets ¹/₄"
from front finished edge.

4. For each grommet placement, cut out the marked opening. Insert the deep side of the grommet through the hole from the garment front; place the ring over the grommet center. Following the grommet pliers manufacturer's instructions, firmly press the grommet and ring in place to attach.

5. Place the jacket on a flat surface with the front edges overlapped in the correct position. Position five buttons on the left side of the jacket front, aligning them with the grommets; mark the center of each button position. Remove the buttons (Figure 3).

Figure 3
Mark button positions opposite grommets.

6. Fold each length of cord in half to form a loop. Place the ends side-by-side at each button placement mark on the jacket front and machine-stitch in place. Sew the buttons in place, covering the cord ends (Figure 4). To close the jacket, insert the loop through the grommet and back over the button.

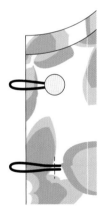

Figure 4
Sew cord ends in place at button locations.
Sew buttons in place over cord ends.

7. Place the closed jacket on a flat surface with the peplum smooth and flat.

8. To stamp the design (see Plan to Stamp first), pour a small amount of textile paint onto the stamp pad. Use the back of a spoon to work it in until the pad is saturated. Lightly tap the floral stamp up and down on the pad until the image is covered but not saturated.

9. Hold the stamp by the edges and press it straight down on the fabric, pushing the stamp evenly with the fingers of your other hand. Lift the stamp straight up; do not slide it as you lift. Stamp designs as desired on the peplum fronts and backs, and on the cuffs. Allow the paint to dry overnight or until it is thoroughly dry.

10. Heat-set by ironing over each image for 30–45 seconds with the hottest setting the fabric will tolerate. Test first on scraps.

11. Mark eyelet positions on the stamped front peplums (but not the back for sitting comfort's sake), using the fabric marking pen to make a dot where each eyelet is desired. Following the eyelet pliers manufacturer's instructions, use the pliers to punch a hole at each mark.

12. Insert an eyelet through the hole from the right side and squeeze firmly with the pliers to attach it to the fabric. ❖

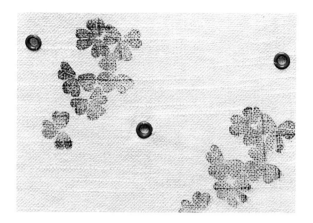

Plan to Stamp

To determine the design placement and test your stamping technique before stamping on the actual jacket:

1. Stamp the design several times on scrap fabric. Use an uneven number of design repeats—three, five or seven, depending on the amount of space to fill. Follow the stamping directions in steps 8 and 9 at left.

2. Make rough cutouts of the stamped designs and arrange them on the jacket pattern pieces for the front and back peplum and the cuff. When satisfied with the design, pin the stamped pieces in place for stamp placement reference on the actual garment.

3. If you are adding colored-eyelet accents, use actual eyelets to plan and mark the placement on the pattern.

Grommets & Eyelets

Not just for functional purposes as originally designed, grommets and eyelets have stepped into the fashion and home decor spotlights in both practical and decorative applications. Both are available in a variety of sizes, and eyelets are also available in myriad colors. Be sure to use the pliers or setting tools that correspond with the grommets or eyelets you purchase and follow the manufacturer's instructions for use. Consider the following ideas for creative applications.

• **Hanging Apparatus:** Don't forget about this traditional use for grommets. It's ideal for shower curtains and window treatments and can be combined with rings, ribbon, lacing, rope and other cords.

• **Closures:** Use grommets or eyelets as shown for the front of a jacket with buttons or toggles and loops. Also apply them to the top edge of a tote bag to create a gathered closure.

• **Embellishments:** Decorate a neckline, cuffs or pant legs with a row of grommets, and then lace with ribbon or cord for a nautical look. For home decor, use grommets or eyelets to embellish pillows or place mats like those shown here, or create two finished fabric squares with grommets around the outer edges so you can lace them together over a purchased pillow.

• **Decorative elements:** Add grommets and/or eyelets in one or varying sizes to embellish fabric for garments, accessories and home decor accents. Apply them randomly or use them to create a letter, flower or other design.

Surface Changes

Textural changes add variety and visual interest to fabric surfaces in the projects that follow. Twist and stitch ribbons, emboss velvet or needle felt on wool. Try tape-resist painting or stitch and slash fabric layers to create a furry chenille texture. These and more fun techniques await in the pages ahead.

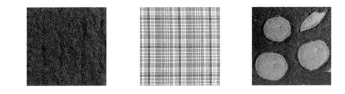

SWEETLY FELTED

Design by Lucy B. Gray

*Craft this easy folk-art bag from recycled old sweaters.
You'll love the intarsia effect created by cutting and fusing
simple shapes of "sweater felt" into the bag body.*

Finished Size
14 x 11 x 3 inches, excluding strap

Techniques
Sweater felting
Intarsia

Materials for Bag
• 3 adult-size recycled 100 percent wool sweaters in
  coordinating colors (such as teal, orange and olive)
• ½ yard 44/45-inch-wide cotton plaid fabric for lining
• ⅔ yard 36-inch-wide tailoring-weight
  fusible interfacing
• 8 x 10-inch piece medium-weight fusible interfacing
• *Optional:* heavyweight fusible interfacing for lining
• Pearl cotton to match sweater fabrics, plus white for
  fruit highlights
• All-purpose threads to match fabrics
• 1 sheet plastic needlepoint canvas
• 12-inch-long zipper
• 16 (½-inch-diameter) buttons in assorted colors
• Scrap paper
• Craft scissors

• Inexpensive shampoo
• Washing machine and dryer
• Press cloth
• Steam iron
• Rotary cutter, mat and ruler
• Basic sewing tools and equipment

Materials for Strap
• Recycled 1-inch-wide belt
• 2 (1-inch-wide) D rings
• 2 (¼-inch-diameter) double-cap rivets
  and rivet setter
• Hole punch for leather
• *Optional:* bench grinder
• Acrylic paint to match belt

Materials for Optional Zipper Pull
• 6–8 large beads to coordinate with lining fabric
  for beaded zipper pull
• Wire cutters (to cut zipper pull)
• Strong cord
• Small lobster-claw clasp

Cutting

- Refer to Make It Felt: Sweater Felting 101 (page 62) to felt the sweaters in your washer and dryer before proceeding with the cutting and bag assembly.
- Choose one felted sweater for the bag body. Cut either two 12 x 15-inch pieces from a crew-neck sweater or one 12 x 29-inch piece from a button-front cardigan sweater as shown in Figure 1. If you use a crew-neck style, the bag will have two side seams. If you use a cardigan, it will have a center-back seam.

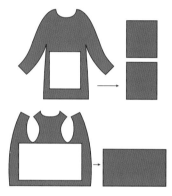

Figure 1
Cut bag pieces from the felted sweater.

Note: You can include the ribbing area of the sweater in the panels. Because the sweater is felted, these areas will be more compact, but still add interesting texture to the completed bag.

- Cut two 16 x 15-inch pieces from both the lining fabric and the tailoring-weight fusible interfacing.
Note: If you want a more rigid bag, cut and fuse two more 16 x 15-inch pieces of heavyweight interfacing to the lining. You will need additional interfacing yardage.
- Cut two 4 x 15-inch pieces of lining fabric and tailoring-weight fusible interfacing for zipper panels.
- Cut two 2½ x 5-inch pieces of lining fabric and tailor-weight fusible interfacing for the strap loops. Cut one 2½ x 29-inch strip of lining fabric for the upper-edge trim.
- Cut two 2 x 14-inch pieces of plastic canvas.

Note: Before proceeding with the bag construction, fuse the tailoring-weight interfacing pieces to their matching fabric pieces, following the manufacturer's directions.

Assembly

1. Copy the orange and leaf templates on page 62 onto scrap paper and cut out. From the two felted sweaters that weren't used for the bag body, cut two large oranges, one small orange and four assorted leaf shapes. Referring to the bag photo on page 56, arrange the felt shapes on the bag front and pin in place. If you cut only one bag piece from a cardigan-style sweater, arrange the felt shapes in the center of the 12 x 29-inch bag piece so they will be on the front of the finished bag.

Note: Cut an extra fruit and leaf shape and practice the intarsia technique first on a scrap of the felted sweater scrap. It's a bit scary to start cutting into the bag body without really knowing the outcome!

2. With sharp scissors, snip into the felt of the bag front underneath one of the pinned fruit shapes. Working from the right side, carefully snip the sweater felt all around the fruit shape. Lift out the double-layer pinned shape. Repeat with the remaining shapes (Photo 1).

Photo 1

3. Unpin each shape from the bag fabric and pat the colored shape into its hole in the bag front. Trim holes as needed for the best fit. Remove the shapes from their holes again.

4. Place the bag piece with the cutouts wrong side up on your ironing board. Insert the oranges and leaves wrong side up into their respective holes. Place the fusible side of the 8 x 10-inch piece of medium-weight fusible interfacing over the inserted pieces with a press cloth on top. Fuse the interfacing to the sweater felt with a hot iron and plenty of steam. The heat and moisture from the iron will felt the wool even more and make the cutouts meld into the bag piece.

5. Working from the right side, use pearl cotton to hand-stitch each cutout to the interfacing below. Use tiny stab stitches around the shapes' perimeters for a terrific folk-art effect. Stitch also around the cut edges in the bag front. With white pearl cotton, stitch a few highlights on each fruit piece with French knots. (Photos 2 and 3).

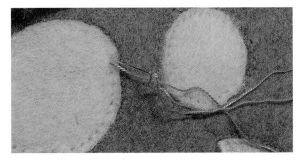

Photo 2

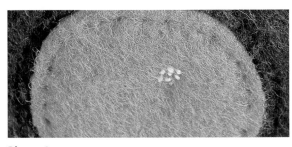

Photo 3

6. If you cut your bag in one piece from a cardigan: Fold in half with right sides facing and short ends even. Stitch ½ inch from the raw edges and press the seam open. Center the seam on the back of the bag and stitch the bottom edges. Press the seam open.

If you cut two bag pieces from a crew-neck sweater, sew the bag front and back pieces together with right sides facing. Use ½-inch-wide seams and stitch together at the side and bottom edges. Press the seam open.

7. Box the bag corners by aligning the side seam line or side center of a one-piece panel with the bottom seam line and press to flatten. Draw and stitch a line 1½ inches from the point, backstitching at both ends. Stitch again ⅛ inch from the first stitching and trim away the triangle close to the second stitches (Figure 2).

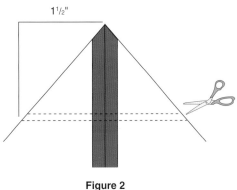

Figure 2
Align side and bottom seam line.
Stitch to box corners and trim.

8. Place both plastic canvas pieces in the bag bottom, and anchor them by sewing through the canvas holes and into the seam allowances at the bag bottom, using a strand of pearl cotton.

9. With right sides together, stitch the two lining pieces together at the sides and bottom edge. Press the seams open. Stitch boxed corners as you did with the bag body. Do not turn the lining right side out. Tuck the lining into the bag and machine-baste the upper edges together ⅜ inch from the raw edges.

10. Fold the two 4 x 15-inch zipper panels in half lengthwise with wrong sides facing and lightly press to crease. Open the pieces and place them right sides together. Measure and mark 1½ inches from each short end with a pin. Stitch on the crease from each end, ending at the pin and backstitching. Fold and press to form the zipper panel (Figure 3).

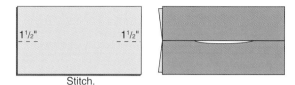

Stitch.

Figure 3
Stitch zipper panels together and press.

11. Pin the closed zipper to one side of the panels, aligning the zipper teeth with the opening in the panels, and stitch all around. Zigzag the raw edges of the panels together all around so that they become one unit (Figure 4).

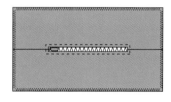

Figure 4
Center zipper under
opening; topstitch in place.

12. Fold the zipper unit in half with the zipper tape showing and stitch ½ inch from the short ends. Press the seams to one side and turn the piece right side out (Figure 5).

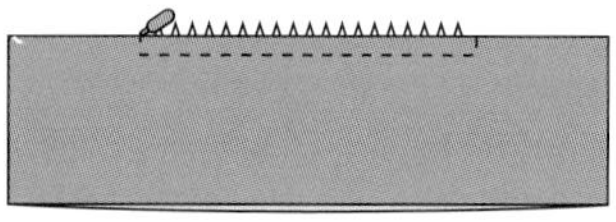

Figure 5
Stitch and turn zipper unit.

13. For the strap loops, turn under and press ¼ inch along each long edge of each of the 2½ x 5-inch rectangles. Fold each one in half with wrong sides together and turned edges aligned. Stitch close to the long edges. Thread each loop through the D rings on the strap, and sew the short ends together ¼ inch from the raw edges (Figure 6).

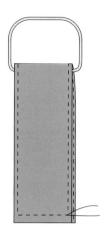

Figure 6
Loop strap through a D ring.
Sew short ends together.

14. Center a loop with ring over a seam allowance at each end on the right side of the zipper unit. Stitch in place ¼ inch from the raw edges.

15. With right sides facing, sew the short ends of the 2½ x 29-inch strip together and press the seam open. With right sides facing and using a ¼-inch-wide seam, stitch the bottom edge of the resulting circle to the outer edge of the zipper unit. Press the seam allowance toward the circle and topstitch ¼ inch from the seam line (Figure 7).

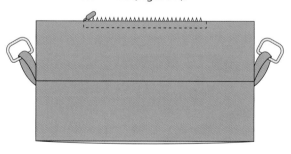

Figure 7
Sew the upper-edge-trim circle to outer edge of
zipper unit. Press seam toward zipper unit; topstitch.

16. *Unzip the zipper.* With right sides facing, pin the upper-edge trim to the upper edge of the bag. Stitch in place using a ¾-inch-wide seam allowance. Turn the upper-edge trim down over the bag edge into the lining and pin in place on the right side of the bag. Turn the loops up and pin in place. Machine-stitch in the ditch of the seam on the outside of the bag, catching the upper-edge trim and the loops in place. Stitch close to the upper edge of the bag, backstitching and stitching forward again to anchor the loop to the bag and hold the upper-edge trim inside the bag in its recessed position (Figure 8).

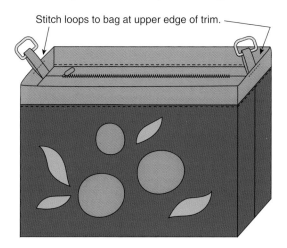

Stitch loops to bag at upper edge of trim.

Figure 8
Stitch in ditch of seam, catching loops in stitching.

17. Evenly space and sew eight ½-inch-diameter buttons to the upper-edge trim on the front and back of the bag.

18. Make the strap following the directions at right.

19. If desired, replace the existing zipper pull with a handmade one. String some colorful beads on several strands of pearl cotton and add a small lobster-claw snap hook. Cut off the old zipper pull with wire cutters and snap the new one in its place (Photo 4). ❖

Photo 4

Strap That Belt

For a strap made from a recycled belt from your favorite thrift store (or purchased on sale or at a discount shop):

1. Cut off the buckle, and using a bench grinder, reduce the thickness of the leather at both ends. This step is not necessary if the leather is thin, but the belt shown was stiff and thick.

2. Punch two sets of holes with a leather punch and touch up the raw leather with matching acrylic paint.

3. Thread a D ring on each strap end and set double-cap rivets in the holes.

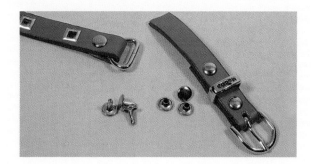

Make It Felt:
Sweater Felting 101

Any sweater that is knitted from 100 percent wool will felt, and some will felt more than others. I've had the best luck felting crew-neck sweaters knit with Shetland wool. This sweater style also yields the most felted yardage since the front and back are simply styled. Raid your own closet for "volunteers" or hit your local thrift shop to find just the right sweater for this project.

Felting wool goes counter to everything you've learned about laundering it. You can expect a 100 percent wool sweater to shrink up to half its size and become very thick and soft using the following method.

1. Set the washing machine for the hottest water temperature and add ¼ cup inexpensive shampoo to the water.

2. Use a 30-minute wash cycle and machine-dry the sweater at the hottest temperature until it is barely damp. Check to make sure it is sufficiently felted. If not, wash and dry again. When the sweater has shrunk sufficiently and is about ¼ inch thick, remove it from the dryer and pat it flat on a smooth surface. Allow to air-dry. The shampoo removes the hard finish that dry cleaning leaves behind on garments and restores a soft, satiny luster to the wool fibers.

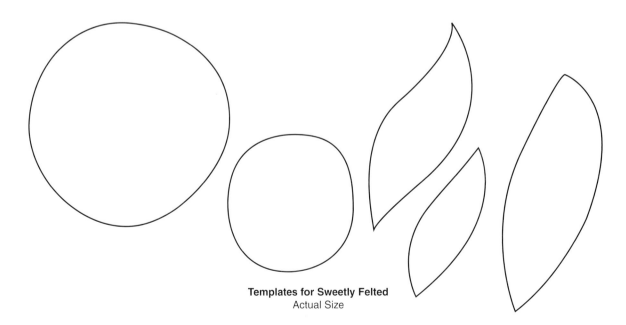

Templates for Sweetly Felted
Actual Size

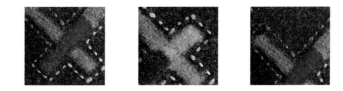

GRAPHIC PUNCH

Design by Pauline Richards

Needle felting by hand or machine is a technique that can open up an entirely new world of creativity for fiber lovers. This classy bag was made by needling wool strips to wool flannel and then outlining the design shapes with multicolored yarn.

Finished Size
8¾ x 10½ x 4 inches

Technique
Needle felting

Materials
• ½ yard sturdy gray wool flannel
• 2 (11 x 14-inch) rectangles lining fabric
• 1 skein multicolor yarn
• ⅛ yard each 4–5 different colors wool fabric
   (colors in the yarn you've chosen)
• All-purpose thread to match fabrics
• Tailor's chalk
• 14 x 25-inch rectangle heavyweight
   nonwoven stabilizer
• 14 x 25-inch piece paper-backed fusible web
• Tapestry needle
• 1 (½-inch-diameter) magnetic snap for purse closure
• 1 (½ x 2-inch) piece thin template plastic
• 1 (1 x 20-inch) ready-made purse strap with rings
• Press cloth
• Steam iron
• Rotary cutter, mat and ruler
• Basic sewing tools and equipment

Special Needle-Felting Tools
• Needle-felting tool and needle-felting mat
OR
• Needle-felting attachment for the Brother PQ 1500
OR
• The Baby Lock Embellisher, a stand-alone needle-
   felting machine
OR
• The Decorative Needlepunch attachment from
   Bernina and a Bernina machine with 5.5mm
   feed systems, including the Activa 125 and
   the Artista 170

Cutting

- From the gray wool flannel, cut one 15 x 25-inch rectangle for the bag.
- From each of the wool colors, cut ½-inch-wide strips in assorted lengths from 1–3 inches, using rotary-cutting tools. You can cut more strips as needed while arranging the pieces on the gray wool rectangle as directed below.
- Use a ruler and tailor's chalk to draw diagonal lines on the wrong side of the gray wool rectangle. Space the lines 4 inches apart (Figure 1).

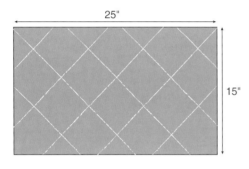

Figure 1
Mark guidelines 4" apart on the true bias.

Needle Felting

1. Referring to Figure 2, center colored wool strips over the drawn lines in the desired combinations. Cut the strips into varying lengths. When you are satisfied with the strip arrangement, pin the strips in place.

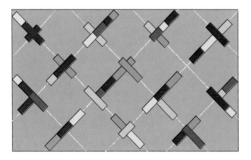

Figure 2
Center strips over lines and pin in place.

2. To needle-felt by machine: Position the prepared fabric under the felting needles. Read your manual, if necessary, before securing the colored strips. Begin felting at the center of the strip, and then work to the left or right, removing pins as you go. Never felt over pins. The strips will shrink slightly as they are felted. By starting in the center and working toward the sides, you will be able to move strips in toward the center as necessary to eliminate gaps in the design. Once all the pieces in a small area have been stitched through, move to the next group of fabric strips and repeat the process. When all fabric pieces have been loosely punched into the base fabric, run the felting needles back over the strips, catching the edges. Stop and check your work by turning the fabric right side up. Look for even color and fiber penetration. Continue felting as needed until you achieve consistent felting and color show-through on the right side of the fabric (Photo 1).

Photo 1

To needle-felt by hand: Position the prepared rectangle wrong side (strip side up) over a felting mat. Adjust the mat so that it is centered under a group of fabric strips. Begin felting (move the felting tool up and down) in the center of the strips and work toward the edges as shown for felting by machine. Remove pins and move strips as necessary to fill in gaps between strips as they develop. Turn right side up, check your work and continue felting individual areas until you are happy with the results.

3. Transfer the felted rectangle to the ironing board and thoroughly steam-press to flatten and shape the rectangle.

4. Use tailor's chalk and a ruler to draw lines ¼ inch away from each felted shape (Figure 3).

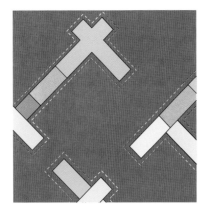

Figure 3
Draw chalk lines ¹/₄" from outer edges
of punched design on right side.

5. Thread a tapestry needle with yarn and do a running stitch around each shape on the chalked lines (Figure 4).

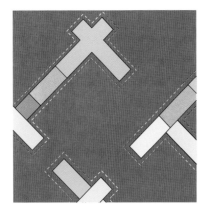

Figure 4
Hand-stitch on chalked lines.

6. Following the manufacturer's directions, apply the fusible web to the 14 x 25-inch piece of heavyweight nonwoven stabilizer. Remove the backing paper and place the piece with the fusible side down on the wrong side of the wool panel. Cover with a press cloth and fuse in place. Press again from the right side, protecting the wool with a press cloth. Trim the rectangle to 14½ x 24 inches.

7. Fold the rectangle in half with right sides facing and mark the shaped side seams as shown in Figure 5. Stitch on the marked lines. Press the seams open. Lightly crease the bottom fold.

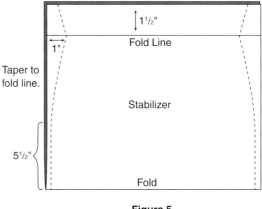

Figure 5
Fold rectangle in half; mark
and stitch shaped side seams.

8. To box the corners, fold the bag so the side seam lines are aligned with the bottom crease. Use tailor's chalk to draw a stitching line 2 inches from the point. Stitch on the line and again ¼ inch from the first stitching. Trim away the point close to the second stitching (Figure 6).

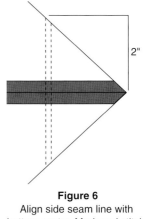

Figure 6
Align side seam line with
bottom center. Mark and stitch.

9. Cut two 1½ x 4½-inch strips from the gray wool. With right sides facing, fold each strip in half and stitch ¼ inch from the long edges. Press the seam open. Turn the resulting tubes right side out and center the seam on the underside of each one; press and edgestitch (Figure 7).

Figure 7
Center seam on underside
of tube. Edgestitch.

10. Slip each tube through a ring on the ready-made strap and fold with the seam on the underside; align the short ends and sew together ¼ inch from the raw edges. Center each strip over a bag side seam and stitch through all layers ¼ and ¾ inch from the upper edge of the bag.

11. On the bag front and back, mark the center 1 inch below the upper edge for the snap placement. Follow the package directions to apply the male half of the magnetic snap to one side of the bag, centering it over the mark and reinforcing it with a ½ x 1-inch piece of thin template plastic. Make slits for the prongs and slip the plastic over them before bending the prongs away from each other and finger-pressing them in place as flat as possible. Apply the female half of the snap to the opposite side of the bag, aligning it with the male half.

12. Prepare the lining by sewing the side and bottom seams as shown in Figure 8, leaving an opening in the center of the bottom seam. Press the seams open and box the bottom corners as for the bag, aligning the side and bottom seam lines. Do not turn the lining right side out.

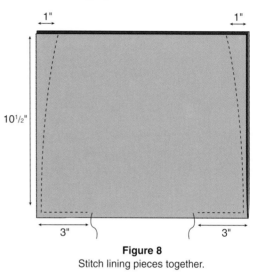

Figure 8
Stitch lining pieces together.

13. Slip the wool bag inside the lining and pin the upper raw edges together. Stitch ½ inch from the upper edge and trim the seam to ¼ inch. Press the seam allowance toward the lining.

14. Turn the bag right side out through the opening in the bottom of the lining. Turn in the opening edges and edgestitch the layers together. Tuck the lining into the bag so the snaps are inside the bag and there is a 1-inch-wide band of the wool on the inside. Topstitch ⅛ inch from the upper edge.

15. For a crisp, permanent shape, firmly press side and bottom creases. ❖

CRAZY FOR CRAYONS

Design by Lucy B. Gray

Remember how much fun it was to color? Bring back that creative childhood experience by coloring cool treats on bleached muslin, and then convert them into pillows by framing them with wacky Log Cabin piecing.

Finished Size
Each pillow: 14 x 18 inches

Techniques
Crayon "prints"
Wacky Log Cabin foundation piecing

Materials for Two Pillows
• 44/45-inch-wide cotton fabric:
  - ¼ yard each 6 different fabrics (plaids, gingham checks, prints and solids in sherbet colors)
  - ¾ yard sherbet-colored plaid for the pillow backs and piecing
  - ⅔ yard black-and-white polka dot for welting and piecing
• 2⅛ yards 36-inch-wide bleached muslin
• All-purpose thread to match or contrast with fabrics
• 2 (16 x 20-inch) pieces white paper
• Template plastic and sharp pencil
• 20 x 32-inch piece low-loft polyester batting
• 1 yard snap tape for pillow-back closures
• 4 yards ¼-inch-diameter cable cord for welting filler
• Black carpet and button thread
• Hand-quilting needle with a large eye (for carpet thread)
• 2 (14 x 18-inch) pillow forms
• *Optional:* several handfuls loose polyester fiberfill
• Spray-on fabric protector
• *Optional:* walking foot

- *Optional:* ¼-inch presser foot
- Rotary cutter, mat and ruler
- Zipper foot
- Iron, ironing board and press cloth
- Basic sewing tools and equipment

Art Supplies

- Crayons (bright greens, yellows, pinks, grays, red, dark aqua and white)
- Acrylic paints (bright pinks and white)
- Artist's brushes
- *Optional:* ice-cream salt
- Paper towels
- Plastic drop cloth or other material to protect work surface

Cutting for Two Pillows

- Preshrink all cotton fabrics and the bleached muslin before cutting the pieces.
- Draw one 14 x 18-inch rectangle on each 16 x 20-inch sheet of paper. Draw a 6 x 8-inch rectangle in the center of each 14 x 18-inch rectangle. Referring to Figure 1, measure and draw in the lines for pieces 9, 8, 7 and 6 in that order.

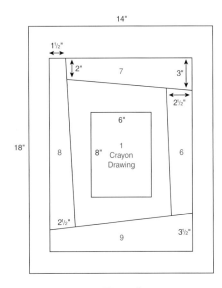

Figure 1
Draw shapes on sturdy paper
using measurements as guides.
(Red numbers indicate piece number.)

- Referring to Figure 2, complete the lines for the inner pieces (5, 4, 3 and 2).

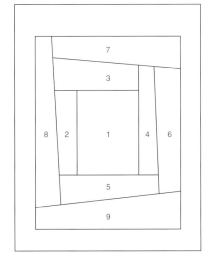

Figure 2
Complete the lines for
pieces 5, 4, 3 and 2.

- Trace shapes 2–9 onto template plastic, adding ¼-inch-wide seam allowances all around as shown for piece 2 in Figure 3. Label each template on the right side with the appropriate number. Use a rotary cutter and ruler to cut each shape from the template plastic.

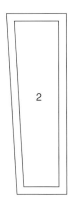

Figure 3
Trace each shape for pieces 2–9
onto template plastic. Add ¹⁄₄"-wide
seam allowances all around.

- From the plaid fabric, cut one 24 x 32-inch rectangle for the pillow back with the lengthwise fabric grain running along the 24-inch length of the rectangle. Cut the rectangle into two 16 x 24-inch pieces. Cut these in half again vertically, yielding two sets of 12 x 16-inch pieces (Figure 4).

Note: *Pin the sets together with the plaids matching so they will still match when you make the pillow backs.*

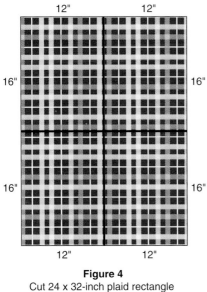

Figure 4
Cut 24 x 32-inch plaid rectangle
into 4 equal pieces.

• On your worktable, arrange the six piecing fabrics, plus the black-and-white polka dot and the remainder of the plaid to determine which one you want to use for each of the eight patchwork pieces surrounding the colored center panel (piece 1). Refer to the pillow photos and notice that the solids are next to prints or plaids for the best contrast. Attach numbered tags to each fabric as a reminder of the piecing order.

• Place each template faceup on the desired fabric for that piece and trace around it twice. Cut out each piece and set the two pieces aside with their template piece on top. Cut two each of pieces 2–9 in this manner.

• From the bleached muslin, cut four 16 x 20-inch rectangles and four 12 x 16-inch rectangles. Cut two 7 x 9-inch muslin pieces for the colored center panels for the pillow tops (piece 1).

• Cut two 16 x 20-inch pieces of low-loft batting.
• From the black-and-white polka dot, cut enough 1¾-inch-wide bias strips to cover 4 yards of cable cord for the welting.

 Note: *Make the welting really dynamic by using that portion of the fabric's design that will stand out when wrapped around the cord. For example, cut polka-dot fabric on the bias so that the dots will be centered on finished welting when the fabric is wrapped around the cord.*

Create the Cool Treats Drawings

1. Center one 7 x 9-inch piece of bleached muslin over one Cool Treats template (see page 77). Trace the image in pencil lightly. Repeat with the second template. Follow the directions that follow to color each one, unless you feel comfortable coloring them on your own.

Note: *If you prefer, draw and color your own images on the muslin or see More Crazy Crayon Options on page 76. Read through the directions to understand the coloring process first.*

2. First test your crayon colors on a scrap of bleached muslin.
To color the gelatin-cube image:
a. Color the whipped cream with the white crayon, really working the crayon's waxy color into the cloth.
b. Add some gray shadow to the lower right side of the whipped cream to give it some dimension.
c. With the white crayon, make a white highlight on the cherry.
d. With a dark pink crayon, color in the cherry. Add dimension with red crayon around the cherry's edge.
e. Pick the lightest yellow-green and color the gelatin-cubes in their centers. With the dark aqua and bright yellow, draw in some of the gelatin-cube outlines. Lightly sketch in the shape of the goblet's sides with gray crayon (Photos 1 and 2 on page 72).

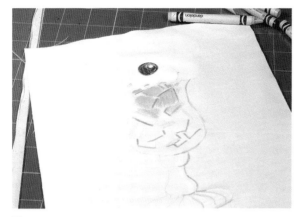

Photo 1

Photo 2

Photo 3

To color the sherbet image:

a. This drawing differs because you are creating the illusion of both glass and metal. It's not more difficult to do—the coloring technique is just more sketchy and impressionistic.

b. Outline the glass dish with a gray crayon. Mix white and pink crayon in a sketchy fashion to color in the bowl.

c. With white crayon, outline the right side of the spoon, and then fill in with gray. You can also use pencil to help define the spoon and features of the glass dish.

d. Use white crayon to create a soft, "out-of-focus" highlight on the sherbet scoops.

e. Color the sherbet scoops with a stippling (dotting) motion, simulating frost on the surface (Photo 3).

3. Place the drawings between several layers of paper towels on your ironing board. Press them firmly with a hot iron (no steam at this point). The goal is to melt plenty of crayon color into the fabric, while blotting excess wax. Notice that the colors have blended and become much richer. If desired, add more crayon color and press again with the iron.

4. Replace the crayon highlights that the hot iron removes by loading a stiff artist's brush with a small amount of white acrylic paint and lightly brushing paint onto the faded highlights. First dab most of the paint onto scrap muslin so the brush is almost dry, and then lightly brush the remainder onto the lightest parts of the drawing—don't overdo it!

5. Place the drawings on a protected work surface. Dip a paintbrush in water and then "paint" the muslin in the area surrounding the crayon image on one piece of muslin. Next, use two colors of pink acrylic paint to paint broad brushstrokes on the wet cloth. Stay clear of the colored images, but notice that the crayon acts as a wax resist to the spreading paint. Some of the paint will migrate into the crayon areas on its own as it dries, adding wonderful texture to the finished drawings (Photo 4).

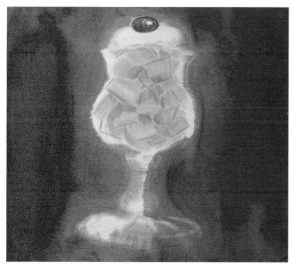

Photo 4

6. If you want to add more texture to the drawings, sprinkle ice-cream salt over the painted surfaces while still wet (Photo 5).

Photo 5

7. Allow several hours for the paint to dry. Rinse the drawings in cool water and allow to dry. Set the paint permanently by pressing the drawings between scraps of muslin with a hot iron and steam.

Pillow-Top Piecing

1. Trim each colored panel to 6½ x 8½ inches, keeping the image centered in the rectangle. Center a colored panel, face up, in the center of each 16 x 20-inch muslin rectangle. Attach the ¼-inch presser foot to your sewing machine. (If you don't have a ¼-inch foot, draw ¼-inch-wide seam lines on the right side around each colored panel.) Machine-baste ¼ inch from each raw edge (Figure 5).

Note: *Begin and end the stitching at the raw edges of the panel, rather than pivoting at the corners, to make sure the panel remains smooth and flat on the muslin.*

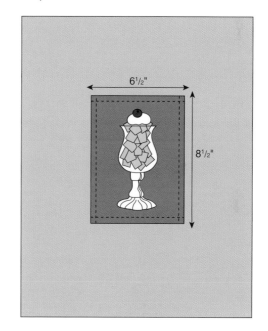

Figure 5
Machine-baste colored panel to muslin
rectangle ¼" from raw edges.

2. If you don't have a ¼-inch foot, use a sharp pencil and a ruler to draw ¼-inch stitching lines all around each piece on the wrong side. Accuracy is important.

3. Position piece 2 right side down on the left-hand edge of piece 1. Stitch ¼ inch from the raw edges (Figure 6 on page 74).

Figure 6
Position piece 2 facedown
and stitch ¼" from edge.

4. Flip piece 2 onto the muslin and press (Figure 7).

Figure 7
Flip piece 2 onto muslin and press.

5. Position piece 3 facedown at the upper edge of the panel with raw edges aligned. Stitch ¼ inch from the edges (Figure 8).

Figure 8
Position and sew piece 3 to upper edge.

6. Flip piece 3 onto the muslin and press (Figure 9).

Figure 9
Flip piece 3 onto muslin and press.

7. Continue in the same stitching-and-pressing fashion to add the remaining pieces in numerical order around the colored panel.

8. For each pillow, make a quilt sandwich with the pieced pillow top on the batting and a second 16 x 20-inch muslin rectangle underneath the batting. Attach a walking foot to your machine if available. Machine-baste ¼ inch from the outer edges of the pieced pillow top through all layers. Trim the excess muslin and batting even with the pillow top.

9. For added design impact, do a hand running stitch through selected fabric pieces of the patchwork using black carpet and button thread and a large-eyed quilting needle (Photo 6). Give both pillow fronts several light coats of spray-on fabric protector, following manufacturer's directions.

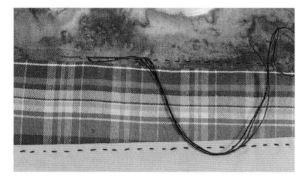

Photo 6

Pillow Assembly

1. Cut the snap tape into two 18-inch lengths.
Note: *For a fun touch, separate the two halves of the tape and paint them in a color to coordinate with the plaid—hot pink in this case. Allow the tapes to dry, and then rinse in cool water to remove excess paint. When dry, steam-set the paint with a hot iron and several layers of paper towels.*

2. Position a muslin piece on the wrong side of each plaid piece and machine-baste in place around the outer edges.

3. Arrange the back pieces on your worktable as shown in Figure 10. Turn under and press ¼ inch at

each opening edge, and then turn under and press ¾ inch. Pin the female side of the snap tape right side up on top of the pressed folds of the bottom piece. Using a zipper foot, machine-stitch along the female tape edges, making sure to catch the edges of the hem underneath.

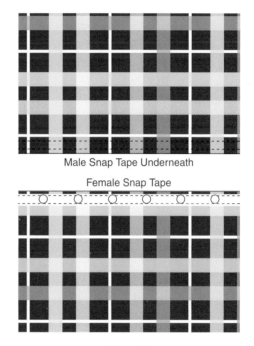

Male Snap Tape Underneath

Female Snap Tape

Figure 10
Turn hems on each panel;
position and stitch snap tape.

4. Sew the male half of the snap tape to the underside of the upper half of the back panel, making sure the snaps and plaid lines match.

5. Snap the male and female tape sides together, joining the top and bottom pieces. Machine-stitch several times over the lapped edges at each long side of the back and treat the joined pieces as one.

6. Sew the 1¾-inch-wide strips together using bias seams. Trim and press the seams open. You should have one 4-yard-long piece.

7. To make the welting, wrap the fabric around the cable cord and stitch close to the cord using a zipper foot (Figure 11). Cut the welting into two equal lengths, one for each pillow.

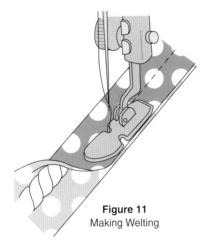

Figure 11
Making Welting

8. Beginning on one long edge of the pillow top, pin the welting to the outer edge with raw edges aligned. Make ¼-inch-long snips into the welting seam-allowance edges at the corners to make stitching easier. Make a neat join where the welting meets itself at the beginning as shown in Figure 12.

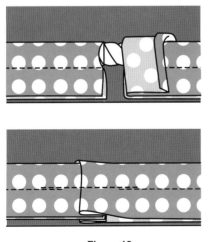

Figure 12
Joining Welting Ends

9. With contrasting thread in the bobbin, stitch close to the cord with the zipper foot.

10. Center the pillow top facedown on the plaid back. Pin in place and stitch just inside the previous welting stitching. Stitch twice over the area where the snap tapes overlap for added strength.

Note: The back is oversize, so make sure the opening is centered and that there are no snaps in the way of the stitching on the long edges. Remove any that are before stitching by cutting the tape around them. After stitching, trim the excess plaid back even with the outer edges of the pillow top. Zigzag the seam allowances together all around the pillow cover.

11. Turn the completed pillow covers right side out through the snap opening and insert a pillow form into each one. If needed, add loose polyester fiberfill in the corners to plump them up. Snap the covers closed and pat the pillows into shape as needed. ❖

More Crazy Crayon Options

If you like the look of crayons on fabric, there are tons more sources of "coloring books." How about clip art, for example? As you probably know, there are literally thousands of copyright-free images available in books and on the Internet. All you need are cartoonlike, simple line drawings. Floral images like these would make darling pillows for a sunroom or porch!

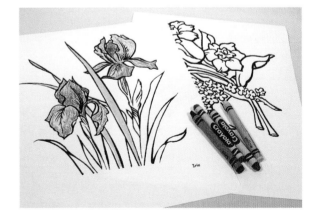

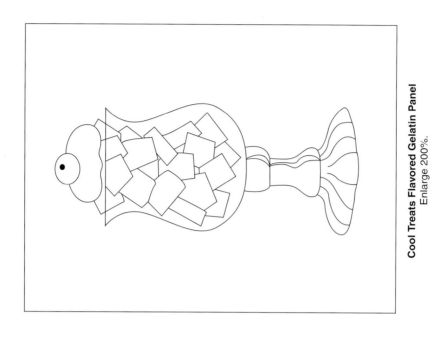

Cool Treats Flavored Gelatin Panel
Enlarge 200%.

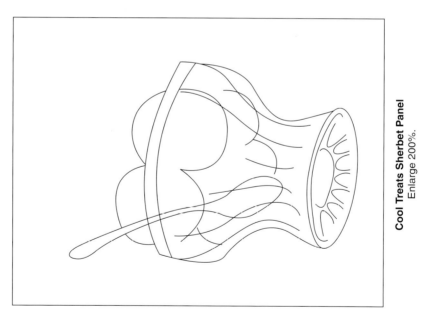

Cool Treats Sherbet Panel
Enlarge 200%.

IRRESISTIBLE GARDEN

Design by Patsy Moreland

Use masking tape and paint to create a lattice backdrop for a garden of appliquéd blossoms with painted accents.

Finished Size
Your size

Techniques
Masking tape resist
Fusible broderie perse appliqué

Materials
- 100 percent cotton or linen unlined ready-made jacket without center-back seam (see Note on page 80)
- ¼ yard each 2 cotton fabrics with large and medium flowers and leaves
- ⅛ yard cotton fabric with butterfly images
- 9 x 12-inch sheets lightweight paper-backed fusible web
- Tailor's chalk or other chalk marker of your choice
- Cardboard
- Waxed paper or plastic wrap
- 1 roll ¾-inch-wide masking tape
- 1 bone folder or wooden craft stick
- ¼-inch-wide synthetic-bristle flat paintbrush
- 1 bottle metallic bronze acrylic fabric paint
- 3 pieces parchment paper
- 1 bottle each dimensional silver and gold glitter paint
- Water container
- Paper towels
- 6-inch-long sharp sewing scissors
- Clear rotary ruler
- Basic sewing tools and equipment

Note: If you prefer, you can make a shirt or jacket instead. In that case, embellish the back and sleeves before assembling the garment.

Preparation & Cutting

• Wash, dry and press the garment and cotton fabric with no additional additives and no dryer sheet.

• Cut a piece of cardboard to fit inside the back of the jacket. Wrap the cardboard with plastic wrap or waxed paper and tape it in place on the back of the cardboard.

• Referring to the manufacturer's directions, apply pieces of paper-backed fusible web to the wrong side of the floral and butterfly fabrics. You can cover each fabric with sheets of the web or you can selectively cut and fuse squares and rectangles of fusible web under the motifs you wish to cut and appliqué to the jacket back.

• Leave the backing paper in place and use the sharp scissors to cut an assortment of flowers, leaves and butterflies from the fabric. Leave on paper backing.

Prepare the Lattice Resist

1. Fold the jacket (or the jacket back piece if you are making the jacket) to determine the location of the center back. Crease lightly, unfold and draw a line from the collar seam line to the bottom edge of the jacket.

Note: For easier taping and painting, undo the side seams and sleeve underarm seams so you can work with the jacket back flat. Reconstruct the jacket after completing the painting and appliqué.

2. Place the wrapped cardboard piece inside the garment with the back of the garment right side up (or work on a flat, waterproof surface if you are making your jacket).

3. Draw a tape placement line 2 inches below the center-back collar seam line perpendicular to the center-back line. Cut a piece of masking tape long enough to reach across the line and align the upper

edge of the tape with the line. Use the bone folder or wooden craft stick to burnish the tape in place—rub it firmly over the tape so that it is securely adhered to the fabric. Cut and center a 19-inch-long strip of masking tape over the center-back line and burnish in place (Figure 1).

Figure 1
Place horizontal tape and then vertical tape (over center back line).

4. Cut 19-inch-long strips of masking tape to create the remainder of the lengthwise resist for the lattice. Place the 19-inch-long strips next to the center strip with edges aligned. Do not burnish. Add strips of masking tape on each side of the unburnished tapes. Carefully remove the unburnished tapes and then burnish the outermost tapes (Figure 2).

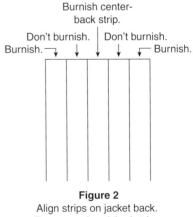

Figure 2
Align strips on jacket back.
Remove unburnished strips.

5. Continue adding vertical tapes until you have added and burnished four pieces of tape to each side of the center tape (a total of nine pieces). On smaller sizes, you may be able to fit only three more strips to each side of the center strip. Referring to Figure 3, cut and add horizontal tapes following the spacing shown. Use a clear rotary ruler to assist in the tape placement to make sure the strips are straight and perpendicular to the vertical pieces. Burnish each tape in place.

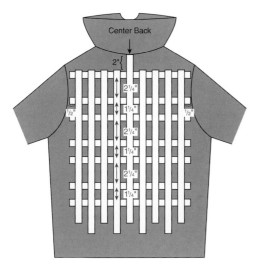

Figure 3
Create lattice on jacket back
with ³/₄"-wide masking tape.

Painting & Appliqué

1. To paint the lattice, apply the bronze metallic paint to the tape edges with the bristle paintbrush. Brush the paint from the tape onto the exposed fabric in the taped trellis (Figure 4). Allow the paint to dry completely before removing the tape. Set the paint following the paint manufacturer's directions.

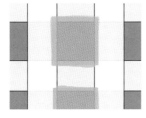

Figure 4
Paint exposed jacket.

2. Tape off and paint designs (triangles, squares or rectangles) on jacket lapels and collar points as desired (see jacket photo).

3. For the sleeve lattice, place a piece of masking tape around the lower edge, with the bottom edge of the tape at the bottom edge of the sleeve; burnish in place. Add a second piece of tape, edge to edge, but do not burnish. Add a third piece of tape, edge to edge. Remove the middle tape and burnish the remaining one. Add 2½-inch-long vertical strips of tape to create the lattice, using the same placement and burnishing method used to create the lattice for the jacket back (Figure 5).

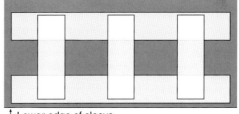
└─Lower edge of sleeve

Figure 5
Tape a grid along lower
edge of each sleeve.

4. Place a piece of wrapped cardboard inside the sleeve and paint each exposed area as described for the back lattice.

5. Remove paper backing from the flowers, leaves and butterflies you prepared earlier. Arrange the pieces on the jacket back over the painted trellis in the desired design. Use large flowers and leaves at the bottom of the lattice, medium ones as you move up the lattice and smaller ones at the top. Position two or more butterflies in the "garden" as desired.

6. When pleased with the garden arrangement, carefully cover the appliqué pieces with sheets of parchment paper and fuse in place following the manufacturer's directions. If desired, add cutouts to the sleeves and/or jacket fronts and fuse in place.

Note: *Do not hold the nozzle above the surface—it must drag on the edge of the fabric to seal the motif to the garment.*

8. Switch to the gold glitter paint and add interior accents on the surface of the appliqués. Allow the paint to dry thoroughly. ❖

7. Remove the screw-top on the silver glitter paint. Place the bottle between your thumb and first finger with the bottle resting on your middle finger. Squeeze the bottle with the first finger so paint comes out of the nozzle. Drag the nozzle along the edge of the fused piece where it meets the jacket fabric. Apply paint to all outer edges of the appliqués. If the nozzle plugs up with paint, stick a straight pin into the hole and push it up and down to release the plug.

OH, WHAT RELIEF!

Design by Pat Nelson

Layers of batting and machine stitching create beautiful dimensional designs in relief when you follow the steps for this noninvasive, machine-trapunto technique.

Finished Size
Your size

Technique
Trapunto by machine

Materials for Lined Vest

- Vest pattern with a plain front or side bust darts in your size
- 44/45-inch-wide medium-weight silk or linen fabric for vest and lining (see Determine Vest Yardage on page 84)
- Thin batting in the same yardage as determined for vest
- ½ yard thick batting for the trapunto design
- Cotton muslin in same yardage as determined for vest
- Buttons as needed for vest
- All-purpose thread to match fabrics
- Rayon or polyester embroidery thread for the trapunto stitching lines
- Water-soluble thread for the trapunto work

- Clear or smoke-colored transparent monofilament thread for background quilting
- Universal needle, size 75/11, and quilting needle, size 75/11, for trapunto and quilting
- Darning foot for your machine
- Water-soluble marking pen
- 4-inch embroidery scissors
- Basic sewing tools and equipment

Determine Vest Yardage

1. To determine required yardage for either vest, do a mock layout on a piece of 44/45-inch-wide fabric using the front and back vest pieces and leaving enough space between the pieces to cut them 1 inch larger than the pattern pieces as shown in Figure 1.

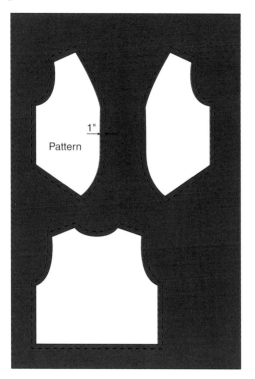

Figure 1
Vest Cutting Layout

2. Use the determined yardage when purchasing the silk or linen for the vest, plus cotton muslin and a lining fabric (the same amount of each).

Cutting

• Do not prewash the vest fabrics.
• Cut the vest fronts and back from the silk or linen fabric, the cotton muslin, the lining fabric and thin batting as shown in Figure 1.

Assembly

1. Refer to Figure 2 for steps 1 and 2. With the water-soluble marker, mark the seam-allowance lines on the right side of the vest pieces. Trace the trapunto designs (page 87) on the right side of the front and back pieces. Arrange the shapes as desired, adding or subtracting flowers and leaves.

2. Place the thick batting on the wrong sides of the vest pieces under the design areas and pin-baste in place around the outer edges of the design, placing pins every ½–1 inch.

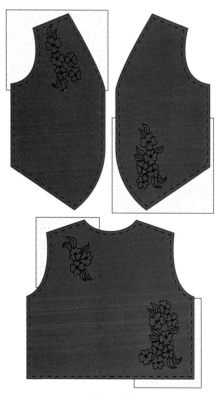

Figure 2
Pin vest pieces to thick batting. Stitch using water-soluble thread in needle and bobbin.

3. Place the darning foot on your sewing machine and lower or cover the feed dogs. Insert the quilting needle and set the stitch length to zero. Using water-soluble thread in the bobbin and in the needle, stitch around each design motif on the outer lines—this is temporary stitching, so it is not necessary to stitch every detail.

4. Turn each piece over and trim away the excess batting just outside the stitching line using the 4-inch embroidery scissors. Trim as close as you can to the stitching line, but do not cut through the fabric.

5. Arrange the vest fabric right side up on top of the thin batting with the muslin underneath and pin the layers together around each stitched design motif. Also pin the layers together every 2–3 inches as shown in Figure 3.

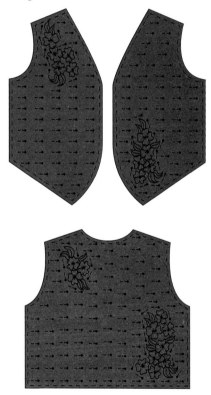

Figure 3
Pin vest pieces to the thin batting
with muslin as the underlayer.

6. Thread the machine with thread to match the vest fabric. Stitch on all design lines of each design motif, including the ones that were stitched with the water-soluble thread. Remove pins as you stitch.

7. Change to monofilament thread in the needle and on the bobbin and stipple-quilt in the open areas

of each vest piece. Using the monofilament thread makes the trapunto design stand out even more.

8. Serge- or zigzag-finish the raw edges of each vest piece. Soak the quilted pieces in cool water to remove the water-soluble thread and marked lines. Machine-wash and dry on delicate. If you are using silk for the vest, hand-wash and line-dry the pieces.

9. Replace the vest pattern pieces on each quilted panel and pin in place. Cut each piece to size.

10. Construct the vest following pattern directions. For an easy lining method, see the lining directions on pages 101 and 102 for the Twist & Stitch vest, disregarding any references to piping. ❖

Oh, What Relief!
Enlarge or reduce shapes to fill the
desired areas on the vest pieces.

HEARTFELT CHENILLE

Design by Carol Moffatt

Stitching rows of straight lines on the bias through two or more layers of fabric and then selectively cutting the stitched channels creates the final quilted and chenille effects in this cute little denim jacket. Chenille heart appliqués add the finishing touch.

Finished Size
Your size

Techniques
Channel quilting
Faux chenille

Materials
- Pattern for a simple, loose-fitting jacket (no darts) with collar in desired size
- 8-ounce, 100 percent cotton denim in twice the yardage requirement listed on the pattern—about 3 yards for most sizes
- All-purpose thread in white or other contrast to the denim color
- Pattern-tracing paper or cloth
- Flathead flower pins
- 6 x 24-inch acrylic ruler with 45-degree angle
- Chalk marker
- Chenille cutting tool of choice: slash cutter or appliqué scissors
- *Optional:* open-toe presser foot for sewing machine
- Lint roller
- Basic sewing tools and equipment

Pattern Adjustments & Cutting

• Read all instructions before beginning.

• Prewash and press the fabric.

• Turn under the hem allowances on the jacket front, back and sleeve pattern pieces, and trace them onto pattern-tracing paper or cloth (Figure 1).

Note: If the front pattern piece has a cut-on front facing, turn the facing under along the front fold line before tracing the pattern pieces. When tracing the jacket back and collar pieces, trace whole rather than half pieces. Be sure to transfer construction marks and the grain-line arrows to the new pattern pieces.

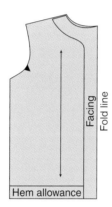

Figure 1
Turn under hem allowance
(and front facing if present).

• Cut out the new pattern pieces. Flip the front and sleeve pattern pieces, pin onto pattern tracing paper or cloth and cut out.

• Fold the denim in half crosswise with selvages aligned and cut the piece along the fold so you have two equal lengths of the fabric with selvages at both long edges of each.

IMPORTANT: Rearrange the two pieces of fabric so the wrong side of the top layer is against the right side of the bottom layer (both pieces are facing right side up).

• Position the new pattern pieces on the layered fabric and line up the grain-line arrows with the true straight of grain (selvage edges). Make sure you have positioned the pieces so you have a left and right front, and a left and right sleeve. Pin in place, allowing at least 2 inches of space between the pattern pieces.

• Cut out each shape, leaving a 1-inch-wide margin of fabric beyond the pattern edges all around. Leaving the pins in place, slip your shears between the two layers of fabric in each piece and trim the upper-most fabric layer even with the pattern edges; leave 1 inch extending all around on the bottom layer (Figure 2). Remove enough pins in each pattern piece so that you can fold it back along the grain-line arrow. Use chalk to draw the grain line along the folded edge of the tissue. Pin the exposed fabric layers together and then remove the remaining pins in the tissue and set the tissue aside.

• Use a few pins to secure both layers of fabric in the remainder of each piece.

Note: Flathead flower pins are the best choice for this step.

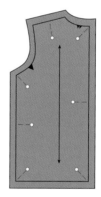

Figure 2
Cut out each piece double-layer with
lower layer 1" larger all around.

Stitching & Cutting the Chenille

1. Refer to Figure 3 for steps 1 and 2. Using the long ruler and the chalk marker, draw 45-degree lines on the top layer of each garment piece. Note that the direction of the angle is different on the left and right fronts, and left and right sleeves (The front armhole has a single notch; the back armhole has a double notch.) On the jacket back and collar pieces, the diagonal lines meet at the center-back line, coming from opposite directions. After establishing the first diagonal line on each piece, measure and mark lines every ½ inch from the first until each piece is covered with lines. Note that the lines extend to the raw edges of the lower layer.

2. Pin-baste the layers together along every fifth line. Adjust the sewing machine for a stitch length of 2.5mm and attach an open-toe presser foot for better visibility. Beginning and ending at the outermost raw edges of each piece, stitch on the first pinned line. On the jacket back and collar, pivot at the center back so each row of stitching is continuous. Remove pins as you sew. Stitch all remaining pinned rows on each piece. Stitch on all remaining lines.

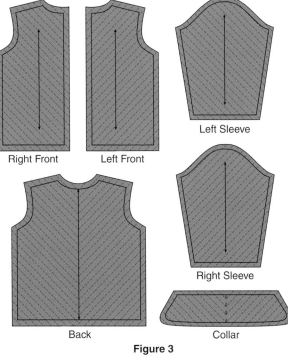

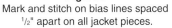

Figure 3
Mark and stitch on bias lines spaced
½" apart on all jacket pieces.

Note: Instead of marking lines on the pieces, you can cut the jacket pattern pieces from Chenille the Easy Way tissues with a preprinted set of diagonal lines spaced ½ inch apart (see page 175 for the source for this product). Use temporary spray adhesive to secure them to the appropriate fabric pieces and stitch on the dashed lines.

3. After stitching each piece, use the chalk marker to draw lines 2⅝ inches from the center front edges and 2 inches from the bottom edges of the top layer of the jacket back, fronts and sleeves (Figure 4). Stitch on the lines, pivoting at the lower front corner on each front.

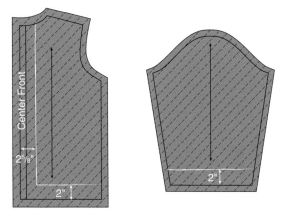

Figure 4
Chalk-mark 2⅝" from center front seam line and 2" from bottom edges on fronts, sleeves and back.

4. Using slash cutter or appliqué scissors, cut through the top layer in each stitched channel on the jacket fronts and back, and the lower edges of the sleeve, ending at the stitching as shown in Figure 5. Slash through the top layer in every stitched channel of the collar piece.

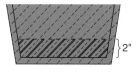

Figure 5
Slash top layer between stitching rows up to stitching line.

5. To prepare the front edges for binding, machine-stitch ¾ inch from the front edges through all layers. Trim away the seam allowance ⅛ inch from the stitching.

6. Pin the original pattern pieces to each piece and cut out each piece. Serge- or zigzag-finish all cut edges of each piece, except the front edges that have just been stitched and trimmed (step 5).

7. Trace the full-size heart templates on page 93 onto pattern-tracing paper or cloth and cut out. Use the pattern to cut four large single-layer hearts and two small hearts from the denim.

8. Pin a large heart to each jacket front as shown in Figure 6 and draw stitching lines with the chalk marker in line with the previous stitching. Stitch on each line, and then slip the cutter between the heart and the top layer of the jacket and slash every stitched channel.

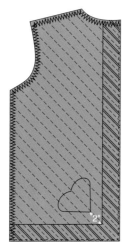

Figure 6
Position large heart on
each front. Stitch on lines.

9. Position two large and two small hearts on the jacket back, mark, stitch and slash as shown in Figure 7. Note the direction of the stitching lines on the large hearts is different from the marked lines on the template.

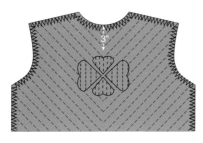

Figure 7
Position and stitch hearts on jacket back.

10. Use the original collar pattern piece to cut an under collar from the remaining denim. Also cut enough 1½-inch-wide true-bias strips to finish the outer edges of the jacket and the sleeve lower edges. Sew the strips together with bias seams to make one long strip (Figure 8).

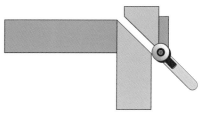

Figure 8
Sew strips together with bias seams. Cut
¼" from stitching. Press seams open.

Jacket Assembly

1. With right sides facing, sew the shoulder and side seams in the jacket and press the seams open. Assemble the sleeves and set into the jacket armholes following the pattern directions.

2. Assemble the collar following the pattern directions, trim the seam, turn right side out and press. Set aside.

3. With raw edges even and ⅜ inch of the bias strip extending from the jacket front edges, pin the bias to the lower edge of the jacket. Stitch ½ inch from the raw edges. Wrap the binding over the raw edges to the inside of the jacket and press. Turn under the raw edge along the stitching line and slipstitch in place. Trim the excess binding even with the front edges of the jacket. Repeat to bind the front edges of the jacket, allowing ³/₈ inch extra to extend at the lower edges. After stitching, turn the extra bias to the inside over the lower edge of the jacket, snugging it to the lower edge, and pin in place. Wrap the bias to the inside and sew in place as you did for the lower edge (Figure 9).

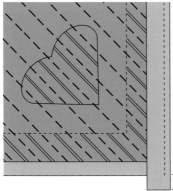

Figure 9
Bind bottom edge.
Then bind front edges.

4. For each sleeve, cut a piece of the bias 2 inches longer than the lower-edge circumference. Turn under and press one end as shown in Figure 10.

Figure 10
Turn under ¹/₄" at one end of bias strip.

5. Beginning close to the underarm seam, pin the bias to the right side of the sleeve. When you reach the folded end, trim away the excess binding strip, leaving enough to cover the turn-under allowance. Stitch, turn, press and slipstitch as you did for the other bindings.

6. Wash the jacket in the washing machine and dry thoroughly in the dryer. To increase agitation that will fluff up the cut edges to create the chenille texture, add old jeans or towels to the loads.

7. Take the jacket outside and shake well to remove excess lint. Also use a lint roller over the chenille areas. ❖

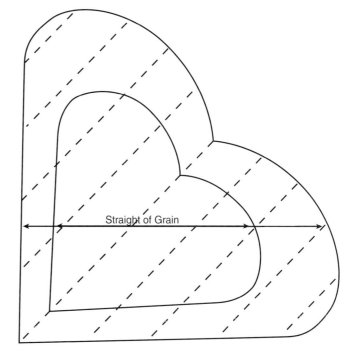

Heartfelt Chenille Templates
Actual Size

RIBBON TWISTS

Designs by Carol Zentgraf

Make an artistic statement with creatively stitched ribbon surfaces. Don't limit this technique to pillow tops. Imagine using it for a vest front, a jacket yoke or an interesting wall hanging. For garments, choose softer, more flexible ribbons to avoid excessive weight and stiffness.

Finished Sizes
Serpentine Twists: 12 x 16 inches
Double Twists: 14 inches square

Technique
Twisted ribbonwork

Materials for Serpentine Twists
• 2 (13 x 17-inch) rectangles jacquard-weave
    decorator fabric for pillow cover
    front and back
• 12 x 16-inch pillow form
• 2½ yards ⅞-inch-wide lightweight ribbon in
    3 different colors to complement your
    decorating scheme
• ¼-inch-wide paper-backed fusible web
• 12-weight cotton thread
• Air- or water-soluble marking pen
• Long rotary ruler or yardstick
• All-purpose thread to match fabrics
• Basic sewing tools and equipment

Materials for Double Twists
• 2 (15-inch) squares solid-color nonwoven faux suede
    or solid-color decorator fabric of your choice
• 1 yard each 3 (2-inch-wide) pin-dot satin ribbons
• 1 yard each 3 (2-inch-wide) solid-color satin ribbons
• ½ yard each 4 (1-inch-wide) pin-dot satin ribbons
• Self-adhesive double-sided basting tape
• 14-inch-square pillow form
• Air- or water-soluble marking pen or tailor's chalk
• Long rotary ruler or yardstick
• All-purpose thread to match ribbon
• Basic sewing tools and equipment

Serpentine Twists Assembly

1. Place one fabric rectangle for pillow front on an ironing surface. Cut a ribbon length to fit across the rectangle diagonally with a little excess ribbon extending past the fabric edges at each edge. Center a length of ¼-inch-wide fusible web on the wrong side of the ribbon and apply as directed by the manufacturer. Remove the paper backing and fuse the ribbon in place across the rectangle. Repeat to cut and fuse ribbon lengths side-by-side in an alternating color pattern to cover the front rectangle (Figure 1). Fuse ribbons in place following the manufacturer's directions.

Figure 1
Cover front pillow rectangle
with ribbons; fuse in place.

2. Using 12-weight thread in the needle and all-purpose thread in the bobbin, stitch through the center of each piece of ribbon.

3. Using the marking pen and ruler, draw a diagonal line across the ribbons from one corner to the opposite corner. Stitch along the marked line, turning down the upper edge of the ribbon before stitching across it (Figure 2).

Figure 2
Turn ribbon edges as you
stitch on diagonal line.

4. Draw parallel stitching lines 3 inches from the first stitching on each side. Rotate the fabric so that when you stitch on each of these lines, the ribbon is turned in the opposite direction from the first to create the serpentine twist (Figure 3).

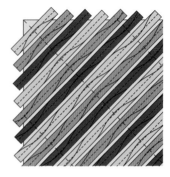

Figure 3
Stitch 3" from first row or stitching, folding
ribbons in opposite direction from the center row.

5. Repeat step 4 to mark and stitch lines 3 inches from the previous ones, folding the ribbon in the same direction as you did for the first row of stitching. Trim the ribbon ends even with the edges of the fabric (Figure 4).

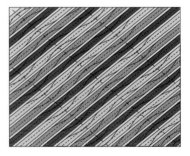

Figure 4
Trim ribbon ends even with fabric.

6. Sew the fabric rectangles together with right sides facing, using a ½-inch-wide seam allowance and leaving an 8-inch-long opening in the center of one long edge for turning. Trim the corners and turn right side out. Turn under and press the opening edges.

7. Insert the pillow form and slipstitch the opening closed.

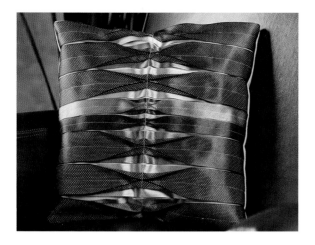

Double Twists Assembly

1. Cut all ribbons into 15-inch lengths.

2. Place one fabric square on a flat surface. Beginning ½ inch from the upper edge of the fabric, position a piece of the 2-inch-wide solid-color ribbon across the square. Arrange two more 2-inch-wide solid-color ribbons next to the first one with edges touching and colors in the order of your choice. Continue adding ribbon strips, positioning two 1-inch-wide pin-dot strips and then three more 2-inch-wide solid-color strips, with the last strip ½ inch from the lower edge of the fabric square. Place a strip of ribbon with dots on top of each positioned strip, aligning the edges (Figure 5).

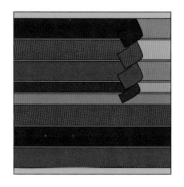

Figure 5
Layer ribbons side by side.

3. Stitch the ribbon layers to the fabric, stitching along the center of the upper ribbon in each stacked pair. Trim the ribbon ends even with the fabric edges. Stitch across the short ends of the ribbons ⅜ inch from the fabric raw edge (Figure 6).

Figure 6
Stitch through center of each ribbon stack and ³/₈" from short ends of ribbons.

4. Use the fabric marker and ruler to draw a line down the center of the panel, crossing the ribbon edges.

5. For each ribbon, cut a narrow strip of basting tape the same distance as the ribbon width. Position the basting tape as shown and fold the ribbon edges in to meet the stitching in the center. Use your fingers to adhere the ribbon to the tape for stitching (Figure 7).

Figure 7
Apply basting tape at center of each ribbon and turn edges toward center.

6. Mark the center again and stitch along the line.

7. Sew the fabric squares together with right sides facing, using a ½-inch-wide seam allowance and leaving an 8-inch-long opening in the lower edge for turning. Trim the corners and turn right side out. Turn under and finger-press the opening edges; do not touch the faux suede with an iron. If necessary to use the iron, use a press cloth.
Note: Use a walking foot to prevent seam slippage and creeping when sewing traditional seams in faux suede.

8. Open the seam of the pillow form and remove enough fiberfill to make a slightly flatter form. Slipstitch the opening closed.

9. Insert the adjusted form through the pillow opening. Slipstitch the opening edges together. ❖

TWIST & STITCH

Design by Pat Nelson

Add crinkles and creases to velvet using an interesting twisting technique to create the fabric for a dressy vest or jacket. The vest shown was made with rayon velvet, but the technique works with many other fabrics. Fusible interfacing on the back of the textured fabric and added stitching control and maintain the textured surface.

Finished Size
Your size

Techniques
Texturizing fabric (also called broomsticking)

Materials
• Vest pattern of your choice
• Rayon velvet (see Yardage Requirements on page 100)
• Lining fabric in yardage given on the pattern envelope
• Woven cotton fusible interfacing (HTC brand is recommended; see Yardage Requirements on page 100)
• All-purpose thread for construction
• Decorative machine-embroidery threads for stitched embellishments
• Size 80/12 universal sewing machine needles for construction; other needles specific to decorative threads as needed

• 4–6 large, strong rubber bands
• Glass-headed pins
• Press cloth
• Basic sewing tools and equipment

Texturizing the Velvet

1. Preshrink the fusible interfacing following manufacturer's instructions. In general, you can preshrink woven fusibles by immersing them in a sink of hot water and allowing them to sit until the water cools. Then hang the fabric to dry.

Yardage Requirements

Use a layout width that is one-third less than the width of your fabric for the following calculation to determine the required velvet yardage. For example, 45-inch-wide velvet will shrink down to about 30 inches after the twisting process. Using this adjusted width, do a mock layout with the pattern pieces for the vest front and back to determine how much yardage you will need. Do not include facings since the vest is lined to the edge. After determining how much fabric you will need, add at least ¼ yard extra.

After you have completed the texturing process, measure the finished width of the fabric; then determine the required yardage for the fusible interfacing using the following formula:

1. Divide the fabric yardage (in inches) by the interfacing width (in inches) to determine the number of interfacing pieces to cut.
3 yards x 36 inches/yard = 108 inches
108 ÷ 22 inches (interfacing width) = 4.9 lengths required (round up to 5 lengths)

2. Multiply the number of lengths required by the fabric width after completing the texturing process.
5 lengths x 30 inches (fabric width after texturizing 45-inch-wide fabric) = 150 inches

3. Divide the results by 36 inches to determine the yardage to purchase.
150 inches ÷ 36 inches = 4.16 yards, rounded up to 4¼ yards of interfacing required

2. Place the velvet in the washing machine and run it through the rinse and spin cycle only.

3. Accordion-pleat the cut end of the wet velvet into 1-inch-wide pleats across the fabric width and secure each end with a rubber band (Photo 1).

Photo 1

4. Step on one of the pleated ends (or have someone hold it for you) and twist the other end with your hands until the piece twists itself into a ball. Use the remaining rubber bands to hold the "ball" together for the next steps (Photo 2).

Photo 2

5. Place the ball near a heat source and allow it to dry. During the winter place the ball on a towel on the warmest radiator or in front of a forced-air register in the house. In the summer, place the ball in a lingerie bag and hang it outside to dry. You can also toss the ball into the dryer, but be prepared for a noisy "ride."

Note: *It's not a good idea to try the drying process in your microwave or conventional oven because burning the fabric is a possibility.*

6. When the ball is dry, remove the rubber bands and carefully open the crinkled fabric. It will naturally unfold to about two-thirds of its original width. With the wrong side up, place the velvet on an ironing board (or a larger padded pressing surface) with the cut edge parallel to the long edge of the board and the excess yardage over the edge in front of you. Using about four glass-head pins, pin the fabric to the ironing board to hold it in place.

7. Cut the interfacing into lengths that match the predetermined finished width of the crinkled fabric. Place the interfacing, resin side down, on the wrong side of the velvet. Evenly distribute the fabric across the length of the interfacing and fuse in place following the manufacturer's directions.

8. Butt or overlap the next piece of interfacing by about ¼ inch and fuse. Repeat until the entire piece of velvet is backed with fusible interfacing, which will preserve the crinkled surface on the right side.

9. Press the finished fabric from the right side using a press cloth to protect the velvet nap and firmly adhere the interfacing.

Vest Cutting & Assembly

1. Cut the vest fronts and back from the interfacing-backed crinkled fabric and from the vest lining fabric.

2. Use decorative threads to embellish the vest pieces with a random pattern of stitching similar to that shown in Figure 1.

3. *Optional: If desired, make faux piping following the directions on page 103.*

4. With right sides facing, sew the velvet vest pieces together at the shoulder seams. Press the seams open. Repeat with the lining pieces.

5. With right sides facing and raw edges even, pin the lining to the vest around the armholes, back neckline and front edges and along the lower edges of the vest fronts and back. Stitch all seams, leaving a 1½-inch-long opening at the center back neckline and lower back edge (Figures 2 and 3) for inserting the ends of the faux piping if you are planning to finish the vest neckline and lower edges with this type of custom-made trim (see Faux Piping on page 103). Pivoting and stitching to the edge at the opening as shown in Figure 3 on page 102 makes it easier to turn in the opening edges accurately.

Figure 1
Do free-form stitching over crinkled velvet pieces
(crinkled surface not shown).

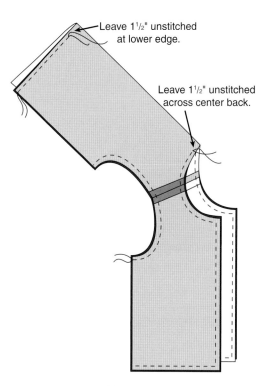

Leave 1½" unstitched at lower edge.

Leave 1½" unstitched across center back.

Figure 2
Sew lining to vest; leave 1½" opening at
center back neckline for faux piping ends.

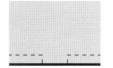

Figure 3
Pivot and stitch to seam edge to leave openings
at center back neck and lower edges.

Note: *If you are using traditional piping, baste the piping to the vest edges before pinning and sewing the lining in place.*

6. Trim the seams to ¼ inch and turn the vest right side out through the shoulders and one of the side-seam openings. Press carefully from the lining side, making sure that the lining doesn't peek out on the right side of the vest at the edges.

7. With right sides facing, and armhole and lower-edge seam lines matching, pin the velvet vest side seams together, with pins starting and ending in the lining at least 1 inch past the seam lines at each end. Stitch the seam, beginning and ending at the pins. This leaves a section of the lining seam to finish by hand at each side seam (Figure 4).

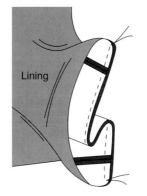

Figure 4
Sew velvet side seams 2" past the
armhole and lower edge into the lining.

8. Turn under and finger-press the seam allowance at the lining front side-seam edges. Pin in place over the lining seam allowance and slipstitch to finish (Figure 5).

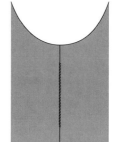

Figure 5
Slipstitch openings in side seams.

9. Topstitch closer to the finished armhole edges to hold the lining in place. If you are not adding faux piping, topstitch close to the remaining outer edges. **Note:** *This step is not necessary if you trimmed the armholes with standard piping trim.*

10. *Optional:* *Add faux piping to the vest front edges and neckline and lower edges following steps 6–10 in Faux Piping below. Topstitch close to all outer edges of the vest if desired.* ❖

Faux Piping

Faux piping is a cord or braid-type trim that is stitched to the finished edge of a garment rather than catching it in the seam-line stitching during the garment construction. That means you can always add piping to a finished edge as an afterthought in the design process. You can use purchased cord trim for this purpose, or you can make your own for a custom look.

The Spinster, a thread-twisting tool, is a must-have for making faux piping for elegant finishing.

Combine a variety of threads and ribbons to make braid to complement the color of the garment. Pearl cotton, embroidery floss, bias-edge silk ribbon and metallic cords and threads are some of the options.

For every yard of faux piping required for the project, you will need about three yards of each of the threads, yarns or ribbons you plan to twist together. Using 3 or 4 strands of size 5 pearl cotton creates a narrow cord for faux piping. For thicker piping, use more strands or thicker cords and yarns. For a more glamorous look, add in some metallic thread or fine cord.

Materials

- 2 different-color skeins size 5 pearl cotton to coordinate with velvet (or other fibers of your choice)
- Clear monofilament thread
- Spinster tool (see Sewing Sources on page 175)
- Open-toe appliqué presser foot
- Hand-sewing thread to match pearl cotton colors

Assembly

1. Cut four lengths, each 3½ yards long, from each of the two colors of pearl cotton. Grasp all threads at one end and tie together in an overhand knot.

2. Attach an end of the thread group to a stationary object; for example, you can place a paper clip around a C clamp on your worktable, and then loop the knotted thread end through the clamp (Photo 1).

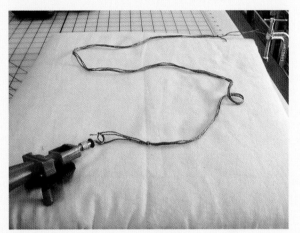

Photo 1

3. Place the other end of the grouped threads into the cup hook on the Spinster tool. Walk away from the stationary thread ends until the thread strands are taut. Then wind the tool until the strands are twisted into a cord and the handle becomes slightly stiff to turn.

4. With your left hand, unhook the threads from the Spinster and set the tool aside. Grasp the twisted threads at their midpoint with your right hand. Bring the two ends together and allow the threads to twist onto and around each other to form the braid (Photo 2 on page 104).

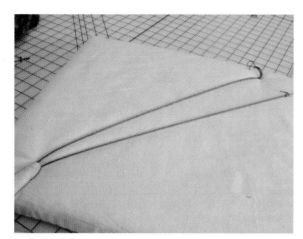

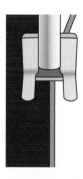

Figure 1
Align cord with garment edge under open-toe
presser foot and zigzag in place.

Photo 2

5. Tie all of the ends together with another overhand knot (Photo 3).

7. Begin attaching faux piping at one end of the opening in the back neckline. Center the garment edge between the open toes under the appliqué presser foot. Place the braid next to the garment edge, leaving a 1-inch-long tail to tuck into the opening later. Begin stitching just below the opening, catching the garment edge in the left swing of the zigzag stitch and catching the twisted cord under the right swing. If you miss a spot, backstitch and go over it again. If you are using Spinster braid, start with the finished end, not the knotted end.

8. Stop stitching about 2 inches from the opening at the lower center back, leaving the needle in the fabric. Determine how much faux piping you need to reach the opening plus 1 inch. Wrap the cord tightly with hand-sewing thread at that length and cut off the excess braid (Figure 2).

Photo 3

Figure 2
Tightly wrap faux piping end with thread.

6. To attach the faux piping to the finished edge of the vest, thread the sewing machine with clear monofilament thread in the needle and the bobbin. Attach the open-toe appliqué presser foot and adjust the machine for a zigzag stitch with a length of 2.5mm and a width setting that will catch the garment edge on the left swing and land in the middle of the faux piping on the right swing (Figure 1).

9. Continue stitching to attach the faux piping. When you reach the opening, tuck the end of the stitched braid and approximately 1 inch of a new braid end into the opening so they cross over each other (Figure 3).

Figure 3
Insert faux piping ends and overlap in opening.

10. Continue stitching across the opening edges, attaching both braids to the garment. When you reach the other end of the opening at the center back neckline, overlap braid ends and tuck inside as you did when overlapping them at the lower edge.

Note: If desired, you can incorporate button loops along the right front edge as you apply the faux piping, using one of the two methods shown below. This method also works with purchased cord or braid trim.

Method One

1. Mark the button position on the left front edge. Measure the button diameter and add ⅛–¼ inch. Experiment with the steps below on a scrap to determine what size loop works best for the chosen button diameter and thickness.

2. Mark the button-loop positions along the right vest front, placing pins for the loop placement of the determined length at the desired button locations (Figure 4).

Figure 4
Mark loop positions.

3. At each loop location, leave a section of the faux piping or cord unstitched, making sure that there is enough slack in the "loop" for the button to slide through easily. When you reach the first pin for the button, backstitch to reinforce the opening. Change

the machine setting to a straight stitch and sew along the fabric edge to the second pin. Return to the zigzag setting, take a few stitches, backstitch, and then continue attaching the faux piping or cord until you reach the next set of pins (Figure 5). Repeat the process for each of the remaining button loops.

Figure 5
Stitch cord to edges,
leaving loop lengths unstitched.

Method Two

1. Mark the button position on the left front edge. Place a pin at the corresponding edge of the right front vest.

2. Make a test loop out of the braid that is large enough for the button to pass through easily, and then measure the amount of trim needed for the loop.

3. Attach the faux piping or cord to the vest front edge with zigzagging until you reach the first pin. Stop stitching with the needle in the vest. Measure out the length determined for the loop in step 2 and form the loop. Pin it in place on the vest edge and continue stitching. Be sure to catch both layers of the loop in the stitching (Figure 6). Repeat to make all remaining loops.

Figure 6
Stitch cord in place, make
loop and continue stitching.

VELVET WRAP-TURE

Design by Pam Archer

Envelop yourself in an irresistible velvet shawl—the perfect accessory for a special evening out. Alternate devoré or burnout velvet with panels of velvet you emboss yourself to create this lovely, one-of-a-kind wrap.

Finished Size
30 x 70 inches, excluding tassels

Technique
Embossing on velvet

Materials
• 36- or 44/45-inch-wide fabrics:
  2⅛ yards solid-color velvet or silk-blend rayon
    for embossing
  2⅛ yards devoré or burnout velvet (leaf or
    floral pattern)
  2⅛ yards firmly woven lightweight lining
    (see Note at right)
• 4 (2-inch-long) beaded tassels

• All-purpose sewing thread to match fabrics
• 3 rubber stamps in coordinating leaf or floral
    motifs for the embossing
• Spray bottle with water
• Rotary cutter, mat and ruler
• Hand-sewing needle
• Silk or cotton embroidery thread for hand basting
• Fine straight pins
• Pinking shears
• Iron
• Basic sewing tools and equipment

Note: *Chiffon was used to line the shawl shown. Its stretchy nature can present handling problems, so it is not recommended for less-experienced sewers.*

Cutting

- Cut three 7 x 70-inch strips from the solid-color velvet.
- Cut two 7 x 70-inch strips of the devoré or burnout velvet.
- Cut one 31 x 70-inch rectangle from the lining fabric.

Emboss the Velvet Panels

Note: To ensure success, read through Embossing Tips & Techniques on the facing page, and the steps below before you emboss the actual pieces for your shawl.

1. Adjust the iron to a medium-high setting and allow to preheat.

2. Place the rubber stamp of your choice right side up on the ironing board.

3. Working on one panel at a time, place a solid-color velvet panel right side down on top of the stamp in the desired position. To avoid cutting into embossed images, make sure that at least ¾–1 inch of fabric extends past the stamp edge when embossing near the cut edges of each panel. You may want to plan the placement for the embossed images on each panel before you begin, and mark the "centers" on the wrong side of the velvet panel with fine pins that you remove prior to applying the iron in the steps that follow.

4. Use the spray bottle to spritz the wrong side of the velvet with water. Position the iron on top of the stamp and apply equal pressure on the iron over the stamp. Be very careful not to move the iron during this process to avoid blurring the images.

5. Carefully lift the iron from the velvet and then remove the velvet from the stamp.

6. Reposition the velvet, alternating stamps as desired and repeating the embossing process until the panel is embossed as desired. Repeat with the remaining solid-color velvet panels until all have been embossed as desired.

Shawl Assembly

Project Notes: *When sewing with velvet, consider its napped appearance since it may cause the panels to appear lighter or darker. To identify the nap direction, run your hand over the surface from one end to the other in both directions along the panel length. In one direction, it will feel rough and in the other smooth. When sewing the panels together, make sure that the nap direction matches from top to bottom so the color is uniform in the finished shawl.*

1. With right sides facing, pin one devoré velvet panel to an embossed velvet panel and hand-baste the layers together ½ inch from the raw edges using a hand-sewing needle and silk or soft cotton thread.

2. Pin and baste the remaining panels to the first pair in alternating fashion to create a 31 x 70-inch rectangle. Remove the hand basting.

3. Carefully press the seam allowances toward the solid velvet panels and pink all seam edges (Figure 1).

Figure 1
Press seam allowances toward embossed panels.

4. Position a tassel on the right side of the velvet panel at each corner as shown in Figure 2. Baste in place.

Figure 2
Baste a tassel to right side at each
corner of pieced velvet panels.

5. With right sides together and leaving a 5-inch-long opening in the center of one long edge, pin the lining to the velvet rectangle along all edges. Hand-baste the layers together, and then machine stitch ½ inch from the raw edges.

6. Remove the hand basting and pink all seams. Turn the shawl right side out through the opening and press carefully, taking care not to put pressure on the embossed motifs (so you won't inadvertently flatten the designs). Turn in the opening edges, pin together and then slipstitch together.

7. Stitch close to the outer edges of the completed shawl.❖

Embossing Tips & Techniques

For the best embossing results, pay heed to the following:

• Be sure that your rubber stamps are very clean. Nothing is more disheartening than adding a color that wasn't planned.

• Test your embossing technique on a scrap to master the technique and build confidence.

• If steam-hole pattern occurs, carefully use the iron's tip to press it out.

• Consider using the pattern of the devoré velvet as a guide for design placement on the solid-color velvet. It will provide you with a designer's eye for motif spacing, angle and frequency of repeats.

• For more color fun, consider applying fabric paint or leftover dye to the rubber stamp before embossing.

BLEACH PLAY

Design by Carol Zentgraf

Use a bleach pen and stencils or stamps to create a design of your choosing on solid-colored fabric. The bleach affects fabric colors differently—some will bleach to white, while others, such as the fabric used for this table runner, bleach to a lighter, different color.

Finished Size
18 x 52 inches, excluding the trim

Technique
Bleach stenciling

Materials
Note: *Read About the Materials on page 112 before you purchase the required materials and supplies.*
• ¾ yard 54-inch-wide cotton decorator fabric
• 1 yard pompom trim
• Coordinating stencils:
    5 x 15-inch design for ends
    1 x 15-inch design for sides

• Stencil adhesive spray
• Clorox bleach pen gel
• All-purpose thread to match fabrics
• Basic sewing tools and equipment

Cutting
• From the decorator fabric, cut one 20 x 54-inch rectangle for the runner.
• Cut the pompom fringe into two equal lengths.

About the Materials

Fabric Selection: Natural-fiber fabrics react best to this color-removal process; some synthetic fibers won't change color at all. It's difficult to predict the result on any fabric before you test it, so it's best to test the bleach on a small piece of fabric before you purchase yardage. Ask for small swatches of fabrics you are considering to test. The time it takes for the bleach to change the color also varies from fabric to fabric.

Bleach: A Clorox bleach pen gel with a writer point on one end and a brush on the opposite end was used for the featured project. Designed for removing spots on laundry, these pens can be found in the detergent and bleach aisle of grocery and discount stores.

Any product that contains bleach will remove color to some extent, but another easy-to-use product is Ultra Clorox UltimateCare Premium Bleach. It's slightly thicker consistency gives you more control over it than regular bleach, yet it's not as thick or cloudy as cleaning solutions containing bleach, making it easier to see what you're doing. You will need a small synthetic paintbrush to apply this type of bleach.

Tools: Stencils and stamps with bold motifs are ideal for creating bleached designs. You can also apply free-hand designs with a round or flat synthetic paintbrush. For stencils, you will need stencil adhesive spray to make certain the stencil edges are firmly adhered to the fabric before applying the bleach.

Bleach Stenciling

Note: *It's a good idea to experiment with bleach stenciling on scraps first.*

1. Spray the back of the larger stencil design with adhesive. Center the stencil on one short end of the fabric with the lower edge of the design 2 inches from the short edge of the runner. Use your hands to press the edges of the cutout areas firmly in place on the fabric.

2. Using the brush end of the bleach pen, gently squeeze the pen and brush a thin layer of bleach gel into each cutout area, using a circular motion. Do not remove the stencil.

3. Leave the stencil in place until the fabric changes color and the bleach is dry. Wipe any excess bleach from the stencil and carefully lift the stencil from the fabric. Repeat for the opposite end of the runner.

4. To stencil the long edges of the runner panel, spray the back of the small stencil design with adhesive. Position the stencil at one end of a long edge with the lower edge of the stencil design 3 inches from the long edge. Follow steps 2 and 3 to stencil the design and let the bleach dry. Repeat to stencil the design along both long edges.

Assembly

1. Turn under and press a double ½-inch-wide hem on all edges of the runner. Stitch in place close to the inner folded edges.

2. Gently rinse the bleached areas with water to remove any remaining gel. Dry and press the fabric.

3. Position the lower edge of the pompom-trim header at the lower edge of each short end of the runner on the wrong side. Stitch in place. ❖

Scribble or Stamp It!

Use the gel pen to do free-hand designs on the fabric or use rubber stamps to apply the bleach in predetermined designs. Just follow these tips for success:

1. Use the brush end of the bleach pen to apply a thin, even layer of bleach to the stamp.

2. Press the stamp firmly onto the fabric and then lift it straight up to avoid blurry edges.

3. Let the bleach dry. Rinse the fabric to remove excess residue.

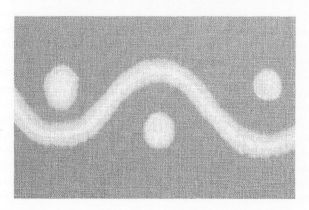

BUTTON FACES

Design by Lucy B. Gray

"Person-alize" an off-the-rack outfit with an eye-catching accessory that turns ordinary craft-store materials into something truly special. Create a "button-face" pin with our copyright-free images and a purchased covered-button kit. Then rearrange silk flower petals for a fantasy flower base; embellish it with bits of ribbon and lace, and voilà!--you have a uniquely styled corsage.

Finished Size
Varies depending on materials

Technique
Photo transfer on fabric

Materials for One Corsage
- 2–3 silk flowers with different petal shapes in complementary colors
- ⅛ yard silk or rayon fabric in a floral or foliage color
- ⅛ yard bleached muslin (preshrink)
- Low-loft polyester batting
- 1 (1⅛-inch-diameter) covered-button kit
- 1 (1½-inch-long) pin back
- *Optional:* 1 sheet white craft felt
- *Optional:* 1 (⅝-inch-diameter) plastic curtain ring
- *Optional:* chenille pipe cleaner for stem
- Needle and thread
- Ribbon, yarn, beads and/or lace and fabric scraps for embellishments
- Air-soluble marking pen
- Fine-point permanent marker
- Lightweight card stock
- Sheets of newsprint
- Fast-drying craft glue
- Spray craft adhesive
- Acrylic paints to match the color of the photo image used (see Printing & Assembly below)
- 1 package florist wire
- Ink-jet transfer paper
- Craft scissors
- Pinking shears
- Iron and press cloth
- 6-inch square wood or similar hard surface that can withstand heat
- Computer, scanner and ink-jet printer (see Note)

Note: You don't need a fancy computer or ink-jet printer to make fabric transfers, so if you don't have one but want to make these corsages, check out Low-Tech Transfers on page 119.

Printing & Assembly

1. Make a color scan of the faces on page 120 at 100 percent resolution and crop out everything except the rows of faces. Save the faces to a file on your computer. With your photo-editing software, open the faces file. Cut and paste multiple rows of the faces into a new file measuring 8½ x 11 inches.

Note: This gives you a full sheet of images to use for additional corsages or for other creative projects and avoids wasting the rest of the transfer sheet.

2. Load your ink-jet printer with a sheet of ink-jet transfer paper and print the new file, following the transfer manufacturer's directions. Allow at least an hour for the inks to dry.

Note: You can also use family photos to make button faces! For one of the corsage shown, I scanned child-hood pictures taken in the 1890s of my grandfather, great-aunt and great-uncle, and then photo-trans-ferred them onto fabric for ⅝-inch covered buttons.

3. Refer to Photo 1 for steps 3–5. Cut the size 45 circle from the back of the button-kit package. Trace its outline onto a piece of muslin. From the sheet of printed faces, cut your favorite face. Lay the face with the image side down in the center of the muslin circle, on top of the wooden square covered with newsprint.

4. Set your iron for dry (no steam) on the "cotton" setting. Cover the circle with the press cloth and firmly press the transfer for about 8 seconds. When it has cooled, gently peel off the paper backing. Allow an hour for the transfer to harden.

5. Center the button front on the wrong side of the muslin transfer. Following the button-kit manufacturer's directions, wrap the button, catching the muslin edges on the little teeth. Tuck all the muslin edges down into the button so the button front and sides are smooth, and then install the button back (Photo 1).

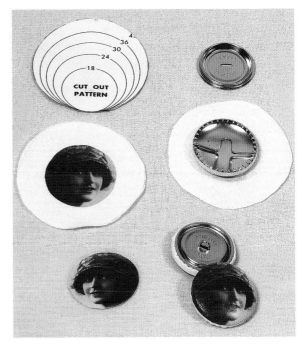

Photo 1

6. Paint the muslin edges of the covered button with diluted acrylic paint in a color that blends with the transferred image colors.

7. If desired, embellish the button with ribbon, yarn, beads and/or scraps of fabric and lace.

8. Cut a few of the flower heads from different stems, and remove the petals by sliding the plastic calyxes off the cut ends of the stems (Photo 2). Use petals that vary in size, color and shape; this creates a more vibrant and interesting arrangement.

Photo 2

9. From fabric scraps, using pinking shears, cut several narrow fabric triangles on the bias. Use your fingers to pull at the pinked edges to "fringe" them. Stack the two largest petals, and then fan the triangles over them with their bases toward the center. With needle and thread, make a few stitches through everything at the center to anchor the arrangement. Continue stacking the petals according to size but alternating the shapes and colors (Photo 3). Hand-stitch all petals together at the centers.

10. Use the leaves from the disassembled flowers, or substitute vintage ones from an old hat. For the Tahitian Girl corsage shown above, collar points from a green shirt were used to create leaves. Hand-baste across the collar a few inches from each collar point and draw up the stitching to gather them into "leaves." Secure the stitches and cut the new leaves from the collar (Photo 4). Stitch them to florist wire that has been folded and wrapped into 3-inch lengths (Photo 5).

Photo 4

Photo 3

Photo 5

11. Add stamens to the corsage to focus attention on the button "centerpiece." Use the ones that came with your silk flowers; because they are plastic, they can be pressed flat with a warm iron and a press cloth. Another option is to tie yarn lengths to a ⅝-inch plastic curtain ring as shown in the center of Photo 6 and glue it beneath the button face. You can also make stamens with a circle of white felt cut 1 inch larger than the button. Make snips toward the center and pull out a few pieces of the "fringe" for a natural look. Paint the felt with diluted acrylic paints and allow to dry (see the circle in the lower right corner of Photo 6). Tuck the snipped-and-painted circle behind the button and glue in place.

Photo 6

12. If your corsage needs a stem, cut a 6-inch length of chenille pipe cleaner and roll it in a 1½ x 6½-inch strip of green fabric. Fold one long edge under, and stitch closed (Photo 7). Curl the stem into a "C."

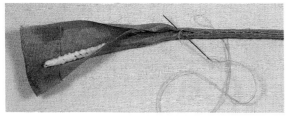

Photo 7

13. Arrange the petals, stamen, button face, leaves and stem (if used) on a 4 x 6-inch piece of card stock. Decide if the corsage would benefit

from more decoration. Try some beads, bits of old jewelry, netting, laces, ribbons and yarns (anything, really). For example, the Belle Époque corsage has vintage netting with chenille puffs glued beneath the flower petals.

14. When you are pleased with the arrangement of the corsage elements, trace the outline of the assemblage on the card stock. Carefully remove everything and set it aside. Draw a free-form line within the tracing as shown in Photo 8. With craft scissors, cut out the smaller free-form shape.

Photo 8

15. Trim the card-stock piece smaller still, so its edges will be at least 1 inch in from the petal outer edges. Note that two "bumps" at the upper edge of the shape were left to support the leaves. Spray the card stock with craft adhesive and add a layer of polyester batting. Trim the excess batting even with the edges of the card stock.

16. Cut one 5 x 7-inch and one 4 x 5-inch piece of the silk or rayon fabric. Place the card stock, batting side down, on the wrong side of the larger fabric piece. With the water-soluble marker, draw a line on the fabric around the card stock, ⅜ inch from the outer edge, and cut the fabric along the line. Make ¼-inch-long snips into the fabric all around as shown in the center image in Photo 9. Lightly dab glue on the fabric tabs and bend them over the card-stock edges. Then lightly dab glue over the anchored tabs and place the backing, tabs side down, on the wrong side of the smaller fabric piece. Weight the backing with a book for several minutes. When dry, trim away the excess fabric. Sign your name and date with a permanent marker (Photo 9).

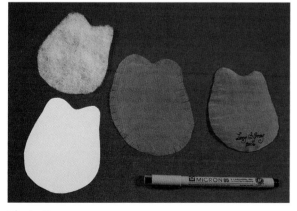

Photo 9

Note: For a backing like the one on the Belle Époque corsage, make a diamond-shaped backing and wrap it with a piece of vintage fabric (this one from a French sample book) or a pretty hanky (Photo 10 on page 120).

Low-Tech Transfers

For this easy method, that doesn't require computer technology, you will need the supplies and embellishments for a corsage as listed on page 114, as well as the following:

• Just-printed color laser photocopy of design image (reversed if needed)
• Transfer medium
• Paintbrush
• Brayer
• Smooth washable surface (picture glass with taped edges works well)

1. Cut the image from the fresh color laser copy. Working on top of the washable surface, use a paintbrush to evenly coat the surface of the photocopy with the transfer medium.

2. Place the coated image facedown on muslin fabric and gently roll it with the brayer. Wipe up any medium exuding at the paper's edges, taking care not to get it on the back of the image. Allow to sit overnight until the image is dry and the transfer is visible through the fabric on the reverse side.

3. Place the fabric and image on a washable surface with the paper side up. Use water to dampen the paper and gently rub it away using a circular motion with your finger. The transfer is delicate when it's wet, so use a light touch when you get down to the image itself. If your image is fuzzy, you haven't removed all of the paper, so keep at it until the image is crystal clear. When the image is completely de-fuzzed, allow it to dry thoroughly.

4. Place the size 45 cutout from the back of the button-kit package under the transferred muslin and trace around it. Cut the muslin circle out and assemble the covered button; then follow the projects directions to create your one-of-a-kind corsage.

Photo 10

17. Dab glue where needed on the back side of the leaves and along the wire leaf stems of your assemblage and position them on the unsigned side of the backing. Hold them in place until the glue has set up. If you made a stem, stitch it in place at the bottom of the backing. Dab glue on the back of the petal cluster and press it onto the backing, on top of the stem and leaves. Wait an hour for the petals

to stabilize, and then glue the stamen in place, followed by the button face. Allow several more hours for everything to dry completely.

18. Glue a pin back to the backing (Photo 11), and attach the corsage to your lapel, a tote bag or your hat. ❖

Photo 11

Scan these face templates at 100 percent resolution and make into photo transfers as directed on page 116.

STITCH IT WITH TWINS

Design by Pauline Richards

Double your sewing fun with twin needles on your sewing machine. Combined with basic and decorative stitching, twin needles instantly transform the silk surface to make the eye-catching patches in this simple but elegant shirt. Transfer the idea to home decor and make large stitched patches or panels for table runners, place mats, pillow tops and comforters.

Finished Size
Your size

Technique
Twin-needle decorative stitching

Materials
- Shirt or unlined jacket pattern of your choice
- Silk, cotton or linen shirting in the yardage specified on pattern envelope plus ⅛–¼ yard extra
- Buttons and notions as specified on pattern envelope
- Interfacing as listed on the pattern envelope
- All-purpose sewing thread to match fabric
- 2 spools rayon or polyester embroidery thread in a color slightly darker than the garment fabric
- Bobbin thread

- Pattern tracing cloth or tissue
- 2mm, 3mm and 4mm size 90 twin sewing machine needles
- Chalk marker
- Lightweight cutaway or heat-away stabilizer
- ¼-inch-wide strips paper-backed fusible web
- Bias pressing bar
- Basic sewing tools and equipment

Cutting

Project Note: *Measurements for the piecing sections on the jacket fronts are for a medium size. Adjust the size of the pieced sections for smaller or larger sizes as needed to create pleasing proportions. You may also need to adjust the section sizes for a more pleasing proportion on other shirt styles and lengths.*

- Trace the shirt front onto pattern tracing cloth or tissue so you have a right and left front pattern piece. Referring to Figure 1 and the project photo, draw horizontal lines on the front pattern pieces to divide them into piecing sections. There are two horizontal lines for the right front and one line for the left front.

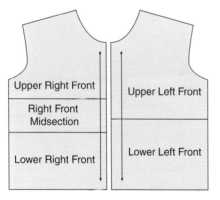

Figure 1
Divide Shirt Fronts into sections.

- Trace the piecing sections onto pattern tracing cloth or tissue and add ⅝-inch-wide seam allowances to the cut edges (Figure 2). Be sure to add straight-of-grain arrows to each piece.

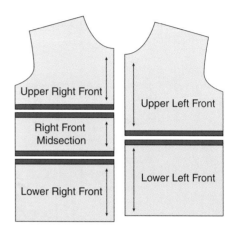

Figure 2
Add seam allowances to cut edges.

- Working on a single layer of fabric, pin the front pattern pieces in place, aligning grain lines. Draw cutting lines 1 inch away from the seam-allowance edges around each piece. Cut out on the chalk lines. You will replace the pattern pieces and trim the pieces to size after doing the decorative twin-needle stitching on each panel.
- Cut the back, sleeves and collar from the remaining fabric as directed in the pattern guidesheet.

Assembly

1. Insert a twin needle in your machine and thread with two spools of embroidery thread. Refer to your sewing machine manual for specific directions for using a twin needle and two spools of thread on your machine. Also read through Twin-Needle Tactics on page 125 before you begin to embellish the individual panels.

2. Back fabric scraps with stabilizer and experiment with the decorative stitches on your sewing machine. Note the stitches and settings you like the best. See Designing Stitches on page 124).

3. Study the direction of the stitched lines in the blouse photo. Use a chalk marker to draw stitching guidelines 1¼ inches apart in the directions shown on each of the front sections.

4. Back each marked fabric piece with lightweight cutaway or heat-away stabilizer. Stitch on the lines with the desired straight or decorative stitch chosen from your stitched samples.

5. Remove the heat-away stabilizer as directed by the manufacturer or trim the excess cutaway stabilizer close to the stitching. Take care not to cut the stitches. Press each piece as needed. Reposition the pattern pieces on the stitched sections, align the grain lines and cut to size.

6. For each front, sew the sections together, press the seams open and finish the seam edges with an appropriate edge finish.

Designing Stitches

• If you are not working with a programmable machine, don't assume that every decorative stitch will work with a twin needle. Choose the desired stitch, insert a twin needle, and then slowly turn the hand wheel to see that the needle clears the throat plate properly. Complete a few stitches by hand before running the machine just to make sure that everything is properly adjusted.

• Experiment with a variety of decorative stitches. When you find a stitch you like, write the stitch number directly on the stitched fabric sample, noting the stitch length and width.

• When using a directional stitch, try stitching odd rows in one direction and even rows in the opposite direction.

• Many stitches are more attractive and appropriate for twin-needle stitching when they are lengthened as much as possible.

7. From the remaining fabric, cut three 1¼ x 20-inch fabric strips on the crossgrain. Fold each one in half lengthwise with wrong sides facing and press. Stitch ⅛ inch from the raw edges to create a tube from each strip. One by one, insert a bias pressing bar into a tube and press the seam open as shown in Figure 3.

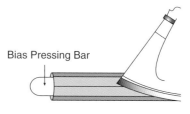

Bias Pressing Bar

Figure 3
Press seam open in center of tube.

8. Remove the pressing bar.

Position and apply a ¼-inch-wide strip of paper-backed fusible web over the seam allowance on each fabric tube. Press to adhere to the tube (Figure 4).

Figure 4
Center fusible web over seam
allowances and fuse in place.

9. Remove the protective paper. Position a tube over each horizontal seam on the fronts and fuse in place following the manufacturer's directions. Stitch close to both edges of each tube.

10. Complete the shirt following the pattern guidesheet directions.

Twin-Needle Tactics

Before starting your twin-needle stitching, read through the following information to ensure success.

• When threading the twin needles, be sure to guide your thread through all thread guides. They help control the tension to prevent excessive wear on the thread, which can cause shredding and breakage, two things you don't want to happen in the middle of a row of twin-needle stitching!

Note: *Many computerized machines allow you to note in the settings when you insert a twin needle. The machine will then automatically limit the stitch width to prevent damage to the needle and the machine throat plate. In addition, you may be able to program in the exact needle width you are using; then the machine automatically increases or decreases the maximum stitch width to accommodate the needle.*

• Clear the area around and behind your machine so that the fabrics can feed smoothly and freely.
• To create smooth, consistent stitches, don't push or pull your fabric. Use your hands to gently guide it and let the machine do the work.
• Sew at a moderate, steady speed for best results. High speeds create excess friction on the thread and result in more thread breakage.
• To prevent missed stitches and broken threads, watch the thread as it travels to the needles. If the thread begins to shred, stop the machine, clip out the damaged section and rethread the needle. Hold both

the cut thread and the new thread in your left hand and begin sewing. When you have finished the row, use a hand-sewing needle to guide the threads to the back of the fabric and then tie the ends to secure.
• If you leave your machine with a section half stitched, note the stitch number, length and width. This information could be helpful if your machine is accidentally turned off before you return to your sewing machine.
• If one thread breaks and you miss only a stitch or two, leave the presser foot down to keep your work accurately positioned and rethread the needle. Resume sewing and go back and fill in the missed stitches by hand.
• If the thread breaks and many stitches are missed by one needle, follow these steps:

1. Stop sewing and remove your fabric from the machine to rethread the needle.

2. Remove all stitches back to the beginning of a stitch pattern.

3. Place a scrap of fabric under the needle, lower the foot and sew slowly until you reach the beginning of the stitch pattern. Stop.

4. Raise the presser foot, remove the scrap and reposition your project fabric so that the needles line up exactly within the pattern. Resume stitching.

5. Pull the thread ends to the back of the work and tie off securely.

ANGEL FELT

Design by Lucy B. Gray

Fused Angelina fibers are the "new felt." Manufactured from spun polyester, these boldly colored, iridescent fibers can be fused together to create a nonwoven sheet that resembles felt but has an interesting sheen. Pick up a few packs of Angelina at craft stores or quilt fairs, or order them on the Internet. Then fire up your iron and your sewing machine and create this fabulous tote in just a weekend!

Finished Size
13 x 15 x 5 inches

Technique
Fiber fusing

Materials
- ¾ yard outer fabric that can be fringed, such as a woven wool
- ¾ yard matching or contrasting lining fabric
- 6 x 24-inch strip nonwoven faux suede for straps
- 2 yards ⅜-inch-wide decorative multicolored or metallic trim
- 1⅓ yards 22-inch-wide heavyweight nonwoven stabilizer, such as Timtex
- 1 crib-size package low-loft polyester batting
- ⅓ yard stiff nonwoven interfacing
- All-purpose thread to match fabrics
- Machine-embroidery and bobbin threads
- 1 sheet plastic canvas for bottom support
- Several packages heat-bondable Angelina fibers: Opal Sparkle, Crystal Mother-of-Pearl, Enchanted Forest, Gold Iris Mix, Calypso Blue and Lemon Sparkle
- Angelina metallic fibers: Magenta Flash, Onyx Flash, Brass Flash and Lapis Flash
- 1 (9 x 12-inch) sheet paper-backed fusible web (such as Lite Steam-A-Seam2)
- 24 black seed beads
- Black beading thread
- Spray-on craft adhesive
- All-purpose craft glue that dries clear
- Parchment paper or Teflon pressing sheet
- Craft scissors
- Spray-on fabric protector
- Iron, press cloth and ironing board
- Rotary cutter, mat and ruler
- Basic sewing tools and equipment

Cutting

- Referring to Figure 1, cut the pieces in the size and shape shown from the material indicated.
- Cut one 4½ x 36-inch strip of heavy stabilizer, one 6 x 37-inch-strip of batting and one 5½ x 38½-inch strip of the outer fabric for the gussets.
- Machine-stitch around the side and bottom edges of the outer fabric pieces to prevent fraying.
- From the lining fabric, cut one 2 x 6-inch rectangle.
- From the plastic canvas, cut one 4½ x 10-inch rectangle for the bottom support.
- From the faux suede, cut two 2 x 24-inch strips and two ¾ x 24-inch strips.

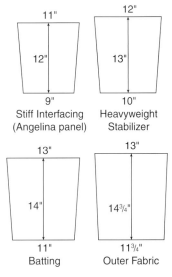

Figure 1
Cut two of each shape from the specified material.

Stiff Interfacing
(Angelina panel)
11" 12" 9"

Heavyweight
Stabilizer
12" 13" 10"

Batting
13" 14" 11"

Outer Fabric
13" 14¾" 11¾"

Making the Angelina Panel

Note: Angelina fibers that are labeled "heat-bondable" will fuse to each other, forming a delicate, feltlike mat. The metallic fibers (labeled "Flash") aren't fusible and must be mixed generously with the heat-bondables in order to stick together. However, they add tremendous sparkle, so be sure to include some in your design.

1. Open the Angelina packages and arrange the fiber bundles on your worktable near your ironing board. Place a 14-inch-square piece of parchment paper (or a Teflon pressing sheet) on your ironing board and preheat the iron to the highest setting, without steam. Pull small tufts of Angelina from the bundles and arrange them as shown in Photo 1 to create a shape that matches the Angelina panel shape you cut from stiff interfacing (see Figure 1). If you are using Flash Angelina, mix these fibers with heat-bondable Angelina before adding them to the composition. Keep the fibers away from the hot iron.

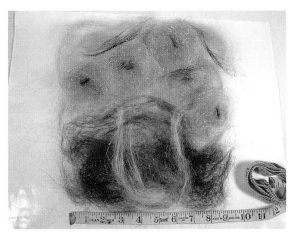

Photo 1

2. Place a second piece of parchment paper (or a second Teflon pressing sheet) over the Angelina arrangement and press for 2–3 seconds with the hot iron (Photo 2). Press just enough to fuse the fibers and no more. Remove the paper or pressing sheet. (If you use too much heat, the sparkle fades and the fibers lose their luster).

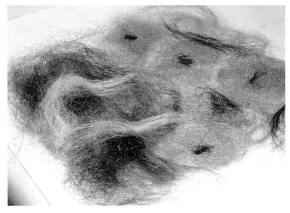

Photo 2

3. At this point, you can add and fuse more fibers onto the design to beef up thin areas or to mix in more or other colors (Photo 3). After fusing the front side of the Angelina "felt," turn it over and press the wrong side, again using parchment paper or a Teflon pressing sheet to protect the fabric and the iron.

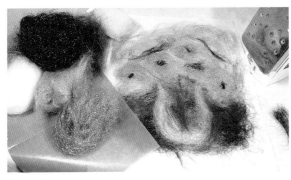

Photo 3

4. When you have finished fusing the Angelina, add some contrast and accents with bits of fabric backed with fusible web. Add small semicircles to the flowers to simulate petal shadows. Cut a few notched strips and fuse inside the vase to make stems. Have a few semicircular petals fall to the table to add more interest to the design (Photo 4).

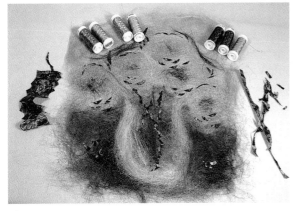

Photo 4

5. Spray the back of the fused Angelina panel with craft adhesive and attach it to the stiff interfacing. With craft scissors, trim away the excess Angelina. If there are some thin patches in the Angelina felt,

lift the mat of fibers from the interfacing and tuck these trimmed pieces underneath to fill in the gaps. Reattach to the interfacing and machine-stitch around the outer edges (Photo 5).

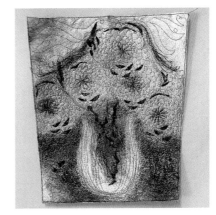

Photo 5

6. Set up your sewing machine for free-motion embroidery (Metafil size 80 needle, darning or embroidery foot, and black bobbin thread in the bobbin). Use embroidery threads in the needle that both blend and contrast with the Angelina. For example, you might use purple, the complement of yellow, to stitch the petals. Free-motion-stitch the entire panel as desired or referring to Photo 6. You'll notice immediately that the stitching causes the Angelina to really come alive. As the surface texture increases from all the stitching, light is refracted from all the little hills and valleys, much in the way a diamond sparkles from its many facets.

Photo 6

Note: If you used Flash (metallic) Angelina and it did not fuse completely, you can "tack" it down now with a light coat of clear-drying craft glue applied with a paintbrush. After the glue has dried, the fibers will still maintain their brilliance.

7. Stitch black seed beads in the centers of the flowers (Photo 7).

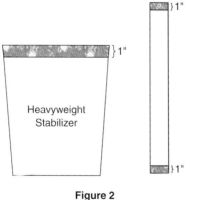

Photo 7

Tote Bag Assembly

1. Apply a coat of spray-on craft adhesive to one side of each piece of heavyweight nonwoven stabilizer, and smooth it in place on the wrong side of an oversized piece of lining. Position so that 1 inch of lining extends at the upper edge of each tote-bag panel and each end of the gusset strip. Place a heavy book on top of each piece for several minutes so that a good bond forms with the lining fabric. Cut away the excess lining, leaving the 1-inch extensions at the top of each piece (Figure 2).

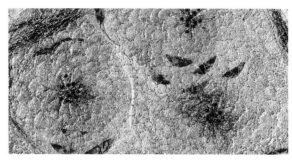

Figure 2
Adhere stabilizer pieces
to wrong side.

2. On the stabilizer, draw a quilting grid, drawing the first line of the grid from the upper right to the lower left corner on each panel. Space the remaining lines 1¼ inches apart. Repeat from the opposite corner to create a diamond grid (Figure 3). Machine-stitch on the lines to quilt the stabilizer and lining together. If you wish to add your own designer label to the lining, stitch it to the upper center of one piece now. Repeat with the gusset panel.

Figure 3
Machine-quilt a diagonal grid on each piece.

3. Test your machine settings by sewing two scrap pieces of heavyweight stabilizer together before you stitch the bag panels to the gusset. With right sides facing, pin the upper corner of one quilted lining/stabilizer panel to one end of the quilted gusset/lining strip. With the gusset on top, stitch ¼ inch from the raw edges. Stop precisely ¼ inch from the lower edge of the tote panel and backstitch. Clip to the stitching and pivot the piece to continue stitching the pieces together (Figure 4). Repeat the clipping and pivoting process at the next corner and stitch the remainder of the gusset to the remaining edge of the lining panel.

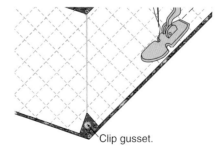

Clip gusset.

Figure 4
Sew gusset to tote lining panel.

4. Hand-sew the plastic canvas to the bottom of the bag as shown in Photo 8.

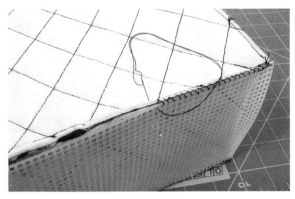

Photo 8

5. Spray one side of the batting gusset with craft adhesive and attach it to the stabilizer over the inside of the gusset with the plastic canvas attached. Fold the excess batting over the front and back panels to cushion the hard edges of the stabilizer. Do the same with the batting panels for the tote bag front and back panels, again folding the excess batting over to the gusset on all sides. Whipstitch all the batting edges to blend them and eliminate ridges.

6. Apply craft adhesive to the wrong side of the Angelina panel and center it on the right side of the front outer fabric piece. Cover the raw edges of the Angelina with decorative trim or ribbon and stitch in place.

7. Using a ⅜-inch-wide seam allowance, stitch the outer fabric gusset to the outer fabric/Angelina panel, right side to right side, as directed for attaching the lining gusset to the lining panels. For the first and last 2½ inches of this seam (at the top of both sides), use a machine basting stitch, but use a regular stitch for the remainder of the seam. This makes it easy to adjust the fit at the top of the outer fabric shell if needed. You can hand-sew these seams back together, if necessary, when finishing the bag. Press all seams toward the gussets.

8. Turn under and press the 1-inch-wide extensions at the upper edge of the tote lining. Slip the lining inside the fabric tote. Check the fit and, if necessary, adjust the seams at the upper edges. To do this, remove the basting stitches from the upper four seams of the fabric tote. You have about a ½-inch leeway at each corner to either let out or take in these seams for a perfect fit. Adjust carefully so the lining lies smoothly inside the tote without buckling or wrinkles. Re-stitch the seams as needed with tiny invisible stitches, or slip the lining out of the tote and re-stitch by machine before reinserting the lining. Hand-baste the lining to the outer shell along its upper turned edge. There will be excess tote extending above the lining at this point (Photo 9).

Photo 9

9. To make the straps, cut two 1 x 24-inch and two ½ x 24-inch lengths of fusible web, piecing as needed. Lay a 1-inch-wide piece in the center of the wrong side of one 2 x 24-inch faux suede strip. Fold the long edges of the faux suede over to meet in the center. Place a press cloth on top, and fuse the layers in place (Figure 5).

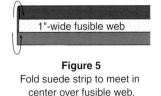
1"-wide fusible web

Figure 5
Fold suede strip to meet in
center over fusible web.

10. Center one ½-inch-wide fusible web strip on top of the fused fold. Lay one ¾-inch-wide faux suede strip right side up on top of the fusible web. Cover with a press cloth, and fuse again (Figure 6). Topstitch the fused strap ⅛ inch from the long edges on both sides. Repeat with the second strap. Give both straps a few light coats of spray-on fabric protector, following manufacturer's directions.

Figure 6
Fuse ³/₄"-wide suede strip on
top of fused strap; edgestitch.

11. Snip the basting thread at the upper edge of the lining inside the tote bag 1 inch from each corner seam and slip the ends of the straps between the layers. Make sure both straps are the same length and the narrow strip of suede on each strap is on the underside. Pin in place. Machine-stitch close to the upper edge of the lining all the way around, catching the straps in the stitching by backstitching and then stitching forward again at each strap.

12. Trim the excess tote bag fabric so that it extends an even ¾ inch above the upper edge of the lining. Carefully remove the crosswise thread to create the fringe around the upper edge (Photo 10). ❖

Photo 10

Angelina Embellished

Embossing

1. Spread an even, thin layer of heat-fusible fibers over a textured surface that can withstand heat. Baskets work particularly well as embossing forms, and there is a tremendous variety of weaves to sample!

2. Place parchment paper or a Teflon pressing sheet on top and press firmly with a hot iron. Work the tip of the iron carefully over the embossing form to get the best imprint.

3. Stitch the embossed image to your project, using free-motion embroidery to accent the pattern even more.

Stamping

Angelina is easily stamped with anything that will hold paint. In the sample shown, wine corks were used with iridescent acrylic paint to add green polka dots to a sheet of Lemon Sparkle Angelina. Experiment with found objects and purchased stamps to create interesting effects on the fused fibers.

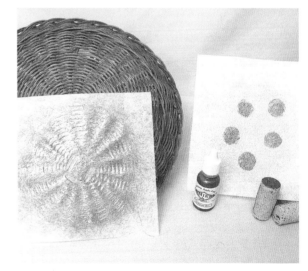

**Embossing and stamping Angelina fibers
accentuates their iridescent quality.**

Patchwork & Appliqué

Patchwork and appliqué are a world unto their own when it comes to embellished clothing and accessories. Make a patchwork jacket or two, appliqué a jean jacket and jeans, even turn aluminum cans into interesting appliqués on a handbag or journal.

A JEANS AFFAIR

Design by Diane Bunker

Jazz up your jeans and a matching jeans jacket with interesting appliqués cut from home decor fabrics and lace. Add a bit of sparkle with Swarovski crystals and you're ready for anything from a casual luncheon to daytime outings to evenings on the dance floor.

Finished Size
Your size

Technique
Machine appliqué
Heat-set crystals

Materials
• Jeans and jeans jacket in your size
• 54–60-inch-wide home decor lace:
    1 yard ecru patterned lace with a noticeable
      design motif easily cut from the background
    ½ yard ecru lace with an allover pattern for
      jacket front yoke
• Assorted large scraps floral and solid-color jacquard-
    style tone-on-tone home decor fabrics
• Paper-backed fusible web
• All-purpose thread to match the denim
• Teflon press sheet
• Clear monofilament thread
• Gold metallic embroidery thread
• Machine-embroidery needles in sizes 75 and 90
• Tracing paper
• Pencil
• *Optional:* Shiva Burnt Sienna Artist Paintstik
• *Optional:* sharp tool
• *Optional:* ½-inch crescent paintbrush
    (Loew-Cornell #247)
• Creative Crystal Pro Tool with 10/ss and 16/ss tips
• Small wire brush to clean Pro Tool
• Swarovski heat-set crystals:
    10/ss Light Colorado Topaz
    16/ss Light Colorado Topaz
    10/ss AB Transparent
    16/ss AB Transparent
• Basic sewing tools and equipment

Appliqué the Jeans

1. Remove the jeans back pockets if you want usable pockets. If you never use the back pockets, you can leave them in place, add the appliqués and stitch in place through all layers.

2. Trace the full-size lace appliqué patterns on page 139 onto paper; cut out and test the shape and fit on the back pockets of your jeans. The two pieces don't have to meet in the middle since they will be covered by a fabric patch. Adjust the size and shape of the two pieces if necessary. Use the paper patterns to cut two of each piece from the patterned lace. Cut matching pieces from the fusible web and apply to the wrong side of each lace piece. Remove the backing paper, position the lace on the pockets, cover with a Teflon press sheet and fuse in place following the manufacturer's directions (Figure 1).

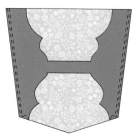

Figure 1
Fuse lace pieces to back pockets.

3. Cut two 3- or 3½-inch squares (large enough to fit on point on the back pockets and cover the lace appliqué raw edges) from one of the floral fabrics. Cut matching squares from the paper-backed fusible web and apply to the wrong side of each square following the manufacturer's directions. Remove the paper, position on the pockets and fuse in place.

4. Thread the machine with clear monofilament thread in the needle and denim-colored thread in the bobbin. Straight-stitch ¹⁄₁₆ inch from the raw edges of each piece. Thread the needle with metallic embroidery thread and adjust the machine for satin stitch. Satin-stitch over the edges of the lace and then over the edges of the floral patches.

Note: At the beginning and end of the satin stitching, drop the sewing-machine feed dogs and stitch in place several times to lock the stitches.

5. Study the photos of the jeans legs for design inspiration. Cut the desired shapes from lace, floral and tone-on-tone fabrics and back each one with a matching piece of fusible web.

6. Remove the backing paper and position in the desired order and arrangement. When you are pleased with the design, top the pieces with the Teflon press sheet and fuse in place. Straight-stitch and then satin-stitch the pieces, working from the bottom layer upward.

Note: Position one design higher on one leg than on the other for more design interest and balance. When stitching the upper design in place, work through the waistline opening over the free arm of your machine. When stitching the lower design, slip the leg over the free arm from the bottom. If the leg won't fit, you may need to partially unstitch the inseam or outseam. Try to avoid unstitching flat-felled seams. In the jeans shown, the outer seam is a normal seam so it would be the one to open.

7. *Optional:* To "antique" the lace, dry-brush it with the Shiva Burnt Sienna Paintstik. This paint dries fast and is permanent when heat-set with your iron following the manufacturer's directions.
a. First remove the protective coating using a sharp tool to scrape it away.
b. Scribble onto a scrap of the protective paper removed from the fusible web.
c. With the paintbrush, pick up some of the paint and softly apply it to the lace. Antique as much or as little of the lace as desired.
d. Heat-set as directed.

Appliqué the Jacket

1. Place a piece of tracing paper on the front yoke and trace the shape exactly. Remove from the jacket and smooth out your traced lines. Add ½-inch-wide seam allowances all around and cut out the yoke front pattern.

2. Cut two jacket front yokes from the allover-pattern lace.

3. Position a lace yoke, right side up, on each jacket front. If the piece must go over a button, cut a small slit just large enough to slip the lace over it. Excess lace will extend past yoke finished edges.

4. Thread the sewing machine needle with clear monofilament thread and stitch the lace in place around all edges as shown in Figure 2. Stitch again ⅛ inch inside the first row of stitching. Trim the excess lace close to the outer stitching.

Figure 2
Place lace on yoke and
stitch. Trim excess lace.

Note: You may use a tiny zigzag for the stitching if you wish. Test on scraps of lace overlaid on denim or similar-color fabric scraps first.

5. Plan the floral and lace appliqué design, apply fusible web, arrange and fuse in place as directed for the jeans appliqués. Straight-stitch and then satin-stitch in the same manner. If you made a slit to fit the lace around a button, hand-tack it in place under the button.

6. Design and apply appliqués to the jacket back as desired. Antique the lace appliqués, if desired, as directed above for the jeans lace appliqués.

Add the Crystals
Use the Creative Crystal Pro Tool to permanently adhere Swarovski heat-set crystals. You will need the 10/ss tip and the 16/ss tip.

1. Screw the 10/ss tip onto the end of the tool, and then plug it in and allow it to heat for a few minutes.

2. Arrange the 10/ss crystals right side up on your work surface.

3. Working on one small appliquéd area of the jeans or jacket at a time, position crystals on and around the outer edges of the appliqués and adjust the positioning until you are pleased with the overall design in that area. The transparent crystals pick up the color of the fabric underneath and are great on the colored appliqués. Use the Light Colorado Topaz and apply to the jeans fabric and in other areas as desired. It's not necessary to duplicate the crystal pattern and placement used on the featured garments.

4. To apply the 10/ss crystals, use the heated tool to pick them up and place them one at a time. Watch the glue melt, and then stick the crystal in place.

Note: If the crystal sticks to the tool instead of the fabric, stick the end of a seam ripper into the slot in the tip to hold the crystal down. This sometimes happens and it means some of the glue has seeped onto the tool. Use the metal wire brush to remove glue from the tip and continue.

5. Unplug the tool and allow it to cool before carefully removing the 10/ss tip and replacing it with the 16/ss tip. Arrange and set the 16/ss crystals as desired.

Note: To protect the crystals during laundering, turn the garments inside out. ❖

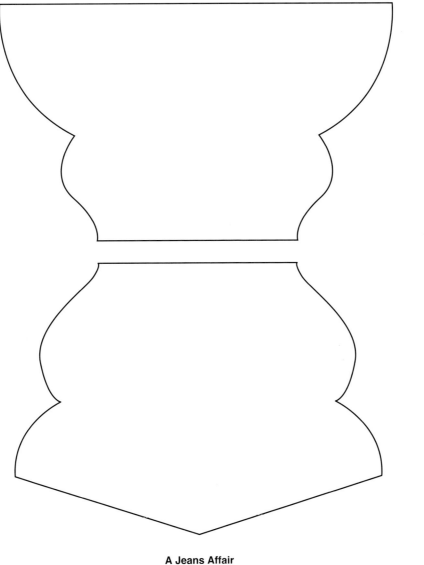

A Jeans Affair
Back Pocket Templates
Actual Size

METAL-SOME STITCHING

Design by Lucy B. Gray

Safely sew metal on a sewing machine? Absolutely! Simple metal shapes cut from soft aluminum soft-drink cans add dramatic visual interest to this roomy ethnic-themed tote bag.

Finished Size
15 x 12 x 3 inches

Technique
Soda-can appliqué

Materials
• 44/45-inch-wide fabric:
    ⅓ yard colorful ethnic print
    ⅓ yard check or plaid
    ½ yard heavyweight lining, such as heavy
        linen or canvas
• ½ yard heavyweight fusible interfacing
• All-purpose thread to match fabrics
• Pattern tracing cloth or paper
• 1 yard fusible fleece
• 9-inch square batting
• 1 pair 5-inch-diameter bamboo handles
• 1 extra-large button for flap front embellishment
• 24–30 ostrich-egg beads, or other flat beads
    with large center holes
• Assorted large bone, metal or wooden beads for
    handle embellishment
• 2 (12-ounce) soft aluminum soft-drink cans
• 2 each ⅜- and ¾-inch-diameter buttons to
    coordinate with bag fabric
• Protective gloves
• 1 magnetic snap set
• 4-inch square milk-jug plastic or plastic
    template material
• 1 sheet plastic needlepoint canvas
• Scrap yarn
• Carpet and button thread to match outer fabrics
• ½ yard hemp or other natural-fiber cord
• Clear-drying, all-purpose craft glue
• Liquid seam sealant
• Air-soluble marking pen or chalk marker
• #5 leather hand-sewing needle
• Size 11 Universal or Sharp needle
• Darning or open-toed presser foot
• Heavy-duty craft scissors
• Craft knife with #11 blade

- Fabric glue
- Kitchen scrubber and dish detergent
- Barbecue tongs
- Flame on fireplace, barbecue grill or propane torch
- Iron, ironing board and press cloth
- Basic sewing tools and equipment

Cutting

- Enlarge the pattern pieces (Figure 1) on pattern tracing cloth or paper and cut out.

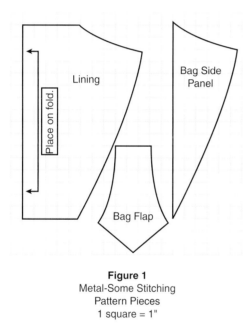

Figure 1
Metal-Some Stitching
Pattern Pieces
1 square = 1"

- Cut two 10¾ x 15¾-inch rectangles from the ethnic fabric and from the interfacing for the bag front and back.
- Using the side panel pattern piece, cut four side pieces on the bias (two right, two left) from both the plaid fabric and the interfacing.
- From the check or plaid fabric, cut two flaps on the bias for the flap and flap facing. Cut two flaps from the fusible interfacing. Cut one flap from the fusible fleece. Cut two 6-inch squares for handle carriers from both the check or plaid fabric and the interfacing.
- Use the lining pattern piece to cut two pieces from both the lining fabric and the fusible fleece.

- Cut one 6½ x 8½-inch rectangle from a scrap of the check or plaid.
- Use the craft knife to cut two 3 x 8-inch pieces of plastic canvas for the bottom support.
- Before proceeding with the construction, fuse the interfacing pieces to their matching fabric pieces to stabilize the fabric and prevent stretching while you work with them.

Metal Appliqués

1. Wearing protective gloves, use heavy-duty craft scissors to cut free the flat side portion of each aluminum can. Be careful because the cut edges are very sharp. Using the barbecue tongs, hold the can pieces over an open flame and allow the flames to "lick" the inside curve of each piece, causing the aluminum to darken and discolor. Allow the pieces to cool; then wash them gently with a kitchen scrubber and detergent to remove the soot.

2. Decide how you will embellish the ethnic fabric with metal appliqués—what shapes, sizes and how many. You can arrange them randomly over the entire surface or in lines or clusters as in the bag shown. Using the craft scissors, cut the desired shapes from the can pieces (Photo 1). Round any sharp edges to prevent unintentional gouges after they have been stitched to the bag sides.

Photo 1

Bag Assembly

1. Adjust your machine for free-motion embroidery, with a darning foot and dropped feed dogs. Use a size 11 Universal or Sharp needle so that the holes punched in the metal will be small. Wear disposable latex gloves when free-motion embroidering; they are flexible and provide full-hand traction when maneuvering the fabric under the needle. Slowly free-motion–stitch the metal shapes to the ethnic fabric pieces in the desired location on the bag rectangle, staying fairly close to the metal-shape edges (Photo 2). When finished, tie off the threads with square knots and trim the threads close. Dot each knot with seam sealant. (This extra little step goes a long way toward keeping the metal shapes from pulling loose later!)

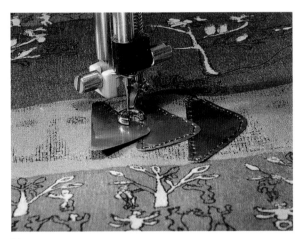

Photo 2

2. Arrange the ostrich-egg beads on the ethnic fabric pieces for the tote (see tote photo for ideas). You might place them in rows or cluster them around a design feature in the fabric's pattern. Coat the wrong side of each bead with a little craft glue; allow several minutes for the glue to harden.

3. Hand- or machine-stitch the beads in place. To machine-stitch the beads and enhance the hand-worked look of the bag:
a. Adjust the sewing machine for free-motion stitching (darning foot and feed dogs dropped).

b. Use your left hand to move the fabric and your right hand to advance the hand wheel—don't use your foot pedal. Insert the needle in the bead hole and then bring the needle up and slide the fabric just enough for the needle to clear the outer edge of the bead.
c. Make one stitch and bring the needle up. Slide the fabric back to allow the needle to make a stitch in the hole again. In this manner—one stitch in the hole, one stitch at the bead's outer edge, back to the hole again—stitch all around each bead (Photo 3).

Photo 3

d. Finish by making two consecutive stitches in the bead hole. Cut the threads 3 inches long, and tie off with a double-square knot on the underside of the fabric.
e. After stitching all the ostrich-egg beads to the fabric, coat each bead lightly with clear-drying craft glue. The glue will keep the thread from wearing through, and prevent your lovely beads from falling off!

4. With right sides facing and using ⅜-inch-wide seam allowances, pin and sew a bias side panel to each long edge of the bag front. Repeat with the bag back. Press the seams toward the side panels temporarily (Figure 2 on page 144).

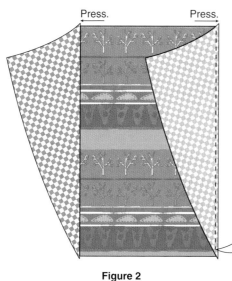

Figure 2
Sew side panels to each ethnic-print panel.

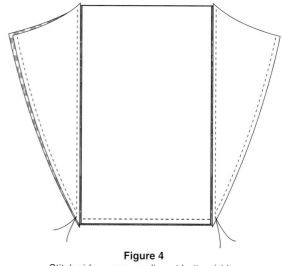

Figure 4
Stitch side seams, ending at bottom/side panel seam intersections.

5. With right sides together, pin the bag front and back together along the bottom edges and stitch from seam line to seam line (Figure 3). Press the seam open.

7. To box the bag corners, align and pin the side seam to the bottom seam at one corner. Press flat with the side seam on top. Measure and draw a 3-inch line perpendicular to the side seam. Stitch on this line, backstitching at both ends. Trim off the point, leaving a ¼-inch-wide seam allowance (Figure 5). Repeat at the other corner.

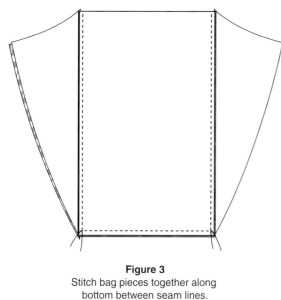

Figure 3
Stitch bag pieces together along bottom between seam lines.

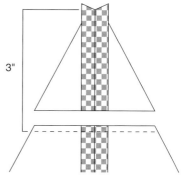

3"

Figure 5
Align bottom and center seam lines. Stitch and trim to box bottom corners.

6. Permanently press the side/front seams toward the center of the tote front and back. Stitch the side seams as shown in Figure 4. Press the side seams open.

8. Make a bottom support by lacing the two plastic canvas pieces together along the outer edges using scrap yarn. Next, wrap the piece in scrap batting and whipstitch the batting edges together. Place the support in the bottom of the bag and anchor to the side seam allowances with a few hand stitches.

9. Serge or zigzag the outer edges of the lining pieces to stabilize them. Trim ⅜ inch from the outer edges of each piece of fusible fleece and apply to the wrong side of each lining piece following the manufacturer's directions. If the fleece doesn't adhere completely in spots, "tack" it down with small dots of fabric glue.

10. Serge- or zigzag-finish the raw edges of the 6½ x 8½-inch plaid or check rectangle for the lining pocket. With right sides facing, turn under 1 inch at one short end of the pocket and stitch ⅜ inch from each side (Figure 6).

Figure 6
Turn and stitch pocket hem.

11. Turn right side out and turn under and press ⅜ inch at the remaining three edges of the pocket (Figure 7). Center the pocket face up on the right side of one of the bag lining pieces with the upper edge 2½ inches below the upper raw edge. Edgestitch close to all but the upper edge.

Note: If you want to add your own designer label, stitch it to the hemmed edge of the pocket now, placing the upper edge of the label ½ inches below the pocket upper edge.

Figure 7
Turn hem to inside. Turn under and press ⅜" on remaining edges.

12. Fold each 6-inch check or plaid square in half with right sides facing and stitch ⅜ inch from the long raw edges, creating a tube. Finger-press the seam open. Turn each tube right side out and press with the seam centered on the underside. Fold each carrier over a bamboo handle with the seam line inside and short ends even. Place a dot of fabric glue on the handles under the carriers, and pin the carriers together close to the handle so the handle cannot move freely (Figure 8). Set aside to dry.

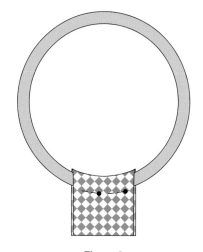

Figure 8
Wrap tube around handle. Pin layers together close to handle.

13. Trim ⅜ inch from the edges of the fusible fleece for the flap before fusing the fleece to the wrong side of one flap piece.

14. Use the pattern for the snap reinforcement on page 148 to cut a piece from clean milk-jug plastic. Use the perforated metal disk that comes with the magnetic snap set as a guide for marking and cutting the vertical slits in the plastic piece and the flap facing. Push the prongs of the male snap piece through the right side of the under flap, the perforated metal disk and the milk-jug plastic, in that order. Bend the prongs to the outside and flatten them.

15. With right sides facing, pin the flap and flap facing together. Stitch alongside the cut edge of the fleece, leaving an opening for turning (Figure 9). Clip corners and points for smoother turning. Turn the flap right side out and press. Slipstitch the opening edges together. Glue a large, decorative button to the flap front.

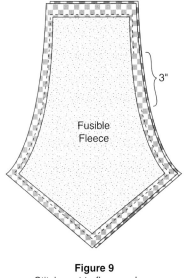

Figure 9
Stitch next to fleece edge,
leaving an opening for turning.

3"

Fusible
Fleece

16. With right sides together and using a ½-inch-wide seam allowance, sew the lining pieces together at the side and bottom edges (Figure 10). Press the

seams open but do not turn the lining right side out. Turn under and press ⅜ inch along the upper raw edge of the lining.

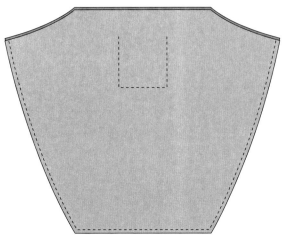

Figure 10
Sew lining pieces together.

17. Box the lower corners of the lining as you did for the tote bag, but stitch 2½ inches from the point (not 3 inches as shown in Figure 5).

18. Turn under and press ⅜ inch at the upper edge of the tote bag. Center the handle carriers on the bag front and back with the lower curve of the handles resting at the upper edge of the bag top; pin in place (Figure 11).

Figure 11
Center bag carrier ends under
upper edge. Pin in place.

19. Temporarily pin the flap back to the center back of the bag with the finished edge 1½ inches from the upper edge (Figure 12).

Figure 12
Pin flap to bag back
1½" below upper edge.

20. Bring the flap through both handles to the bag front and use an air-soluble marking pen to draw around the flap point to mark the position. Lift the flap slightly and mark the position of the snap on the bag front. Unpin the flap and set aside.

21. Cut a 2-inch square of milk-jug plastic. Using the perforated disk for the remaining half of the snap, mark and make two slits in the plastic. Center the perforated disk on the snap positioning mark on the bag front and mark and make the two slits. Install the female snap part in the same way as the male part (Photo 4). Dab some craft glue on the snap prongs and pad them with a small square of scrap batting.

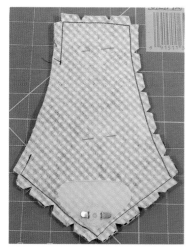

Photo 4

22. Slip the lining into the tote bag with seams and upper turned edges aligned. Thread a leather hand-sewing needle with 12 inches of carpet and button thread. Hand-stitch the lining and outer fabric together, ⅛ inch from the top edges (rethreading the needle as needed). Because the layers are thick and you are striving for a handworked look, sew with small stab stitches (where the needle pierces both layers in a single, perpendicular pass, back and forth, back and forth. You'll have several layers to pierce at the handle carriers, but the leather needle makes the stitching so much easier (Photo 5). Hide the thread knots between the two layers.

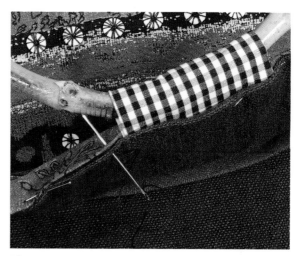

Photo 5

23. Attach the flap back with button sets as follows:
a. Join the male magnetic snap part to the female part on the bag front.
b. Thread the flap back through the handles and pin it to the bag back.
c. Position one ¾-inch button in each lower flap corner and place a pin through one of the holes in each button. Carefully unfasten the magnetic snap.
d. Double-thread the leather hand-sewing needle with carpet and button thread. Stitch the buttons in place, catching a ⅜-inch button in place inside the bag with the stitches to reinforce the attachment (Photo 6 on page 148). Tie the threads off on the lining side, and dot with seam sealant.

Photo 6

24. Complete the ethnic theme of your bag by tying a handle "charm" to one of the bamboo handles. You can find genuine African bone and metal beads at bead shops or in the chain craft stores. String several on lightweight cord and tie them above one of the joints in the bamboo handle (Photo 7). ❖

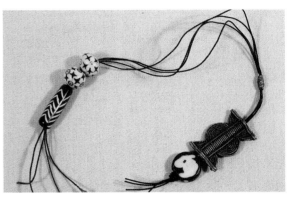

Photo 7

Snap Reinforcement Template
Actual Size

A Metal-Some Book

This soda-can–appliqué technique also works for other projects! Try covering purchased blank books with interfacing-backed fabric appliquéd with metal shapes. Measure the front cover of the blank book and cut fabric and interfacing slightly smaller. Fuse the interfacing to the fabric, and then add beads and the metal shapes just as you did for the Metal-Some Stitching bag. Finish the edges with a dense zigzag or satin stitch. Coat the wrong side with a thin layer of all-purpose craft glue and press onto the book front cover. Pad it with a towel and place under heavy books for a day to allow the glue to dry.

CIRCLE UP!

Design by Pam Archer

Satin-stitched circles of organza with stitched embellishments and ribbon accents add up to a handcrafted, one-of-a-kind wearable to pair with your favorite jeans or skirt. Using an existing garment makes this a quick-to-stitch-and-wear project.

Finished Size
Your size

Technique
Machine appliqué

Materials
- Purchased cotton shirt or unlined jacket in your size (washable)
- ¼ yard each assorted 36- or 45-inch-wide silk organza fabrics to complement and coordinate with your shirt or jacket
- Water-soluble stabilizer
- *Optional:* Temporary spray adhesive
- 6–7 yards total ¼-inch-wide variegated and ¼- or ⅜-inch-wide satin ribbons in your choice of colors
- 40-weight embroidery thread in colors to coordinate with and complement the organza fabrics and the ribbons
- Tailor's chalk
- *Optional:* Open-toe embroidery/appliqué presser foot
- Rotary cutter, mat and ruler
- Basic sewing tools and equipment

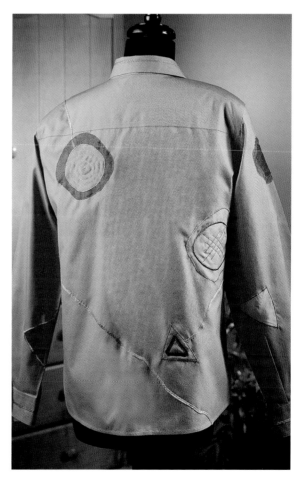

Cutting

• Launder the shirt and the organza fabrics and press to remove wrinkles.

• Using the templates on page 152 as a size and shape guide, cut assorted circles and triangles from the organza fabrics. Cut two of each shape of the same color, cutting one on the crossgrain and one along the lengthwise grain of the organza so the grain lines will be in opposite directions when you layer them. This helps prevent stretching and distortion.

• Cut extra shapes and sizes so you have plenty to work with to create a pleasing arrangement on the fronts and back of the garment.

Embellishing the Shirt

1. Use tailor's chalk to draw a ribbon placement line through the center of the collar and each cuff.

2. Hand-baste or use a light coat of temporary spray adhesive to adhere a 1-inch-wide strip of water-soluble stabilizer underneath each line. Cut and pin a piece of variegated ribbon in place along each traced line, turning under and pinning the raw ends for a neat finish. Machine-baste through the center of the ribbon with matching thread.

3. *Optional: If you like to wear your collar up and cuffs turned back, cut a piece of matching or contrasting ribbon for each one. Center the ribbon over the machine basting on top of the stabilizer on the underside of the collar and cuffs and machine-baste in place.*

4. Adjust the machine for a medium-length zigzag stitch, just wide enough to stay inside the ribbon edges. If available, attach an open-toe embroidery/appliqué presser foot. Use thread on top and in the bobbin to match the ribbon colors. Sew the ribbon(s) in place (Figure 1). At each turned end, shorten the stitch length and stitch several stitches in place to secure them. Carefully tear away the stabilizer on the underside.

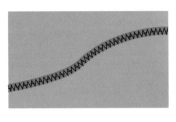

Figure 1
Zigzag trims in place.

5. Now the fun begins. Arrange the organza pieces as desired on each garment section, mixing and matching shapes and colors. For the best effect, use double layers of each shape and size and rotate the grain line to control stretching (Figure 2). Baste the double-layer shapes together before positioning them on the garment. Refer to the project shown for ideas, but don't limit yourself to the colors, shapes and arrangements shown. Try on the garment to check the final placement of the shapes and adjust as needed.

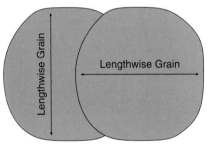

Figure 2
Stack pieces in pairs with grain lines perpendicular to each other.

6. Remove the shirt and draw couching lines for ribbons with tailor's chalk as desired to complete the planning process. Leave the shapes pinned in place if desired. However, it's easier to add the ribbons without the shapes attached. Make a sketch of the placement or take a digital photo to print out for reference. Before removing the organza shapes, draw around each one with tailor's chalk.

7. Working on one garment section at a time, cut and position strips of stabilizer under the couching lines. Baste or use temporary spray adhesive to attach the strips. Cut and then position and stitch

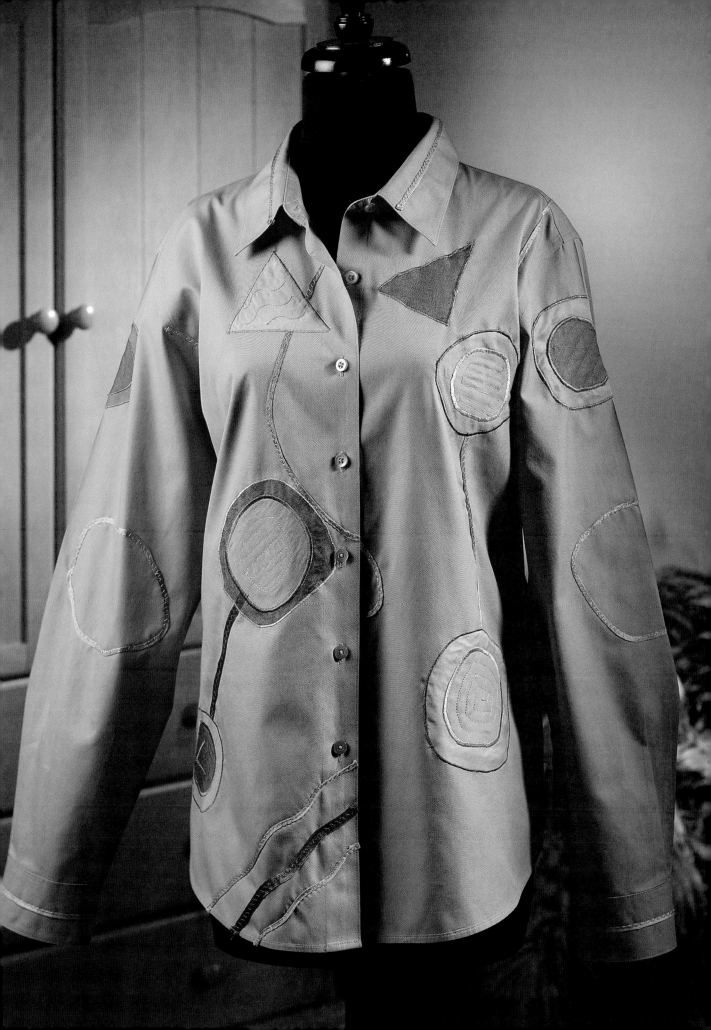

your choice of variegated and satin ribbons in place over each line as directed for the collar and cuff ribbon embellishments.

8. Replace the organza shapes, one by one, and add a square of stabilizer to the underside, making sure to cut it larger all around than the shape you are attaching. Use temporary spray adhesive to hold the shapes and stabilizer in place or baste through all layers close to the outer edge using thread that blends into the organza color. Satin-stitch each shape in place (see Sensational Satin Stitching

below). If desired, use straight or decorative stitches to further embellish the innermost shapes in each stack of organza pieces. ❖

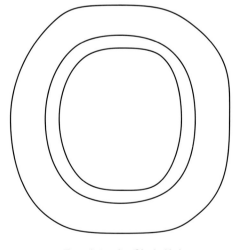

Sensational Satin Stitching

For sensational satin stitches, opt for rich, dense zigzag stitches and colorful embroidery threads.

1. With the design and stabilizer pinned in place, machine-baste around the outer edges to hold the shape in place.

2. Attach an embroidery foot or zigzag foot and set the machine for a satin stitch of the desired width and density. For machine appliqué, satin stitching is done with a very short stitch length so the stitches lie side by side and cover the fabric edge underneath.

3. Experiment with stitch settings on scraps first. In the project shown, most of the larger outer circles were sewn with a short, narrow stitch (.3mm long x 2.0mm wide), while a slightly wider stitch (.3mm long x 4.0mm wide) was used for the smaller center circles.

4. Position the fabric raw edge under the center of the presser foot. Stitch around the outer edges of the appliqué to encase the raw edge in stitching. Remove the cutaway stabilizer.

Test varying stitch widths on scraps first.

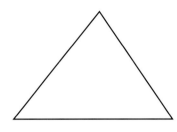

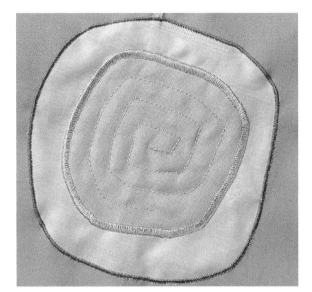

Templates for Circle Up!
Actual Size

Pointers for Perfect Stitching

When satin stitching around a square outside corner, stop the needle in the fabric on the outer edge of the appliqué. Rotate the fabric 90 degrees and resume stitching, sewing over the previous stitching at the corner (Figure 1).

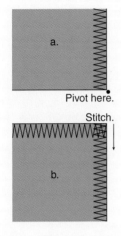

Figure 1
Satin Stitching a Corner.

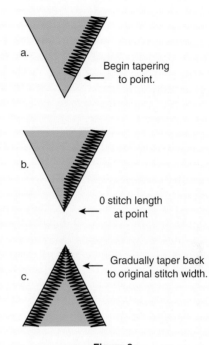

Figure 2
Satin Stitching to a Point

To satin-stitch around sharp points, refer to Figure 2. This technique prevents lumps and unsightly, loose satin stitches that hang off the points.

1. Stitch toward the point and stop stitching when the width of the remaining point is the same width as the satin stitch (a).

2. Continue stitching, stopping often to gradually decrease the stitch width so that it is 0 when you reach the point (b).

3. Leave the needle in the fabric and pivot. Continue stitching, gradually increasing the stitch width to match the original width (c).

For smooth curves, stop every few stitches with the needle in the fabric on the outside edge of the curve. Lift the presser foot, rotate the fabric slightly, drop the foot and continue stitching in this manner (Figure 3).

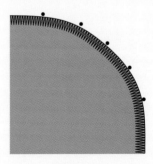

Figure 3
Stop every few stitches (see dots) at edge of appliqué; pivot slightly. Continue stitching.

DOUBLE UP

Design by Carol Moffatt

This simple reversible vest is accented with a Celtic Key appliqué on each side with colors in reverse. An interesting double-layer, raw-edge appliqué technique makes this an easy project that's quick to stitch and doubles your wearing options. Try it on a simply shaped jacket or adapt the design and the idea for casual pillows.

Finished Size
Your size

Technique
Raw-edge appliqué

Materials
- Simple cardigan-style vest or jacket pattern with a straight front edge
- Lightweight woven cotton fabric (red cotton Osnaberg shown) in the vest yardage listed on the pattern envelope
- Lightweight polyester knit fleece (black) in the vest yardage listed on the pattern envelope, plus ½ yard for appliqué and binding
- ¾ yard 44/45-inch-wide lightweight cotton T-shirt knit in color to match the woven fabric; there will be extra fabric left for another project
- All-purpose thread to match the woven and fleece fabrics
- ½ yard tear-away paper or stabilizer
- Pattern tracing cloth or paper

- Carbon paper
- Pencil
- Appliqué scissors
- *Optional:* open-toe appliqué presser foot; ¼-inch presser foot
- Basic sewing tools and equipment

Pattern & Fabric Preparation

• Prewash all fabrics and press as needed to
  remove wrinkles.
• Make any required fitting adjustments to the vest
  front and back pattern pieces to accommodate
  your figure. Set the facing pieces aside; you will
  not need them.

*Note: The key pattern is designed to fit the front edge
of a vest that finishes to 20 inches from neckline edge*

*to bottom edge. Check the length of your pattern
piece and adjust it as needed. For larger sizes or
when a longer vest is desired, create the Celtic Key
pattern as directed below, adding one or more key
repeats as required so the key fits the vest front
length as desired.*

• At the lower edge of the adjusted vest front
  and back pattern pieces, turn under the hem
  allowance and pin in place.
• Trace the adjusted front and back vest pattern
  pieces onto pattern tracing cloth or paper. Mark
  the armhole seam lines on the front and back
  pattern pieces. Cut out the pattern pieces, cutting
  away the armhole seam allowances along the
  seam lines you drew on the pattern pieces.
• Cut four 6 x 21-inch strips of tear-away stabilizer
  and two 6 x 21-inch strips of carbon paper (or
  longer if necessary for the design to fit along your
  vest front).
• Enlarge the Celtic Key pattern on page 159 onto
  one strip of the tear-away to create Key One (and
  adding additional key motifs as required if your
  pattern is longer).
• This project requires a total of four key pattern
  pieces, two for Key One and two reverse images
  for Key Two. To create them in one step, refer to
  Figure 1 and stack the Key One pattern with the
  remaining strips of tear-away and carbon in the
  order shown. Make sure all edges are aligned and
  pin or clip the layers together.

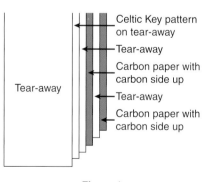

Figure 1
Stack strips as shown.

• Use a pencil to trace the design, pressing hard so that lines transfer from the carbon paper onto the tear-away layers. Remove and discard the carbon paper. As a result of tracing the design in the stacked layers, you will have two strips of Celtic Key One and two of its reverse, Celtic Key Two.

Cutting

• Cut the vest front and back pattern pieces from the woven fabric and from the fleece.
• From the fleece, cut two 6 x 21-inch strips (or longer for longer key strips on longer vests) with the length of the strips parallel to the selvage. Repeat with the T-shirt knit.
• For the contrast shoulder and side-seam finish on the woven side of the vest, measure the shoulder and side seam lengths on the pattern piece; add the results and add 2 inches. Cut two ½-inch-wide strips of fabric this measurement, cutting them parallel to the selvage so they won't stretch.
• Set the remaining fleece aside for the binding for the armholes and bottom edge.

Applying the Appliqué

1. Beginning with the right front vest piece cut from the woven fabric (red), pin the Key One tracing on tear-away to the wrong side, 2 inches from the center front cut edge and 1½ inches below the front neckline cut edge. Repeat with the left front and Key Two (Figure 2).

Figure 2
Pin Celtic Key strips to
wrong-side vest fronts.

2. In the same area, on the right side of the vest front, position and pin a strip of the fleece, textured side up. Make sure that the strip extends past the tracing lines on the tear-away on the wrong side.

3. On the wrong side, pin through all layers around the appliqué lines, making sure that all three layers are anchored together and are wrinkle-free.

4. Adjust the sewing machine for a normal straight stitch length (2.5mm). Attach an open-toe appliqué presser foot or other foot of your choice that allows for each viewing of the traced lines on the tear-away. Thread the machine with thread in a color to match the fleece color. Stitch along the Celtic Key lines on the tear-away, pivoting carefully at the corners and removing pins as you go (Figure 3). When you reach the point where you started stitching, change the stitch length to 2mm and continue for an additional inch. Clip the threads. Carefully remove the tear-away.

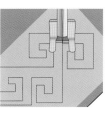

Figure 3
From right side, stitch on the Celtic
Key design; pivot at corners.

5. On the right side, use an appliqué scissors to trim the excess appliqué fabric close to the stitching—about ⅛ inch from the stitching. If desired, trim even closer after the first trimming.

6. Repeat the appliqué steps above to add the T-shirt–knit (red) appliqués to the right side of the fleece (black vest fronts).

Assembly

1. With right sides facing, sew each vest back to its corresponding fronts at the shoulder seams and press the seams open.

2. On the woven-fabric (red) vest only, center a ½-inch-wide strip of fleece over each shoulder seam. Attach the ¼-inch presser foot (or draw a stitching guideline through the center of each strip). Stitch through the center of each strip to attach to the vest (Figure 4). Sew the side seams of each vest and add strips to the side seams of the woven-fabric vest in the same manner.

Figure 4
Center black fleece strip over
shoulder seam. Stitch through center.

3. With right sides facing, pin and sew the two vests together along the neckline and center front edges, leaving the armholes and bottom edges unstitched. Trim the seam allowances to ¼ inch; turn the vest right side out and press from the woven-fabric side. Adjust the machine for a straight stitch with a length of 3mm and topstitch ⅛ or ¼ inch from the finished edges.

4. Pin the vest layers together around the armholes and along the bottom edges. Make sure both layers are smooth and wrinkle-free with no pulls. The raw edges may not match. If they don't, trim so they do. Stitch ¼ inch from the raw edges and remove the pins.

5. Measure the bottom edge of the vest and add 2 inches. Use this measurement to cut a 2-inch-wide lengthwise strip from the fleece for the bottom-edge binding. If necessary, cut two or three strips and sew together with bias seams. Press the seams open.

6. With right sides facing, raw edges even and excess strip extending past both front edges, pin the strips in place. Stitch ½ inch from the raw edges (Figure 5).

Figure 5
Sew strip to bottom edge.

7. Wrap the binding strip over the raw edge to the fleece side of the vest and pin in place. Stitch in the ditch of the seam on the woven side to catch the binding on the fleece side (Figure 6). Trim the excess binding close to the stitching on the fleece side, and trim excess binding even with the finished front edges of the vest.

Figure 6
Stitch in the ditch from right
side to catch fleece on inside.

8. Measure one armhole and add 1 inch. Use this measurement to cut two 2-inch-wide binding strips along the lengthwise grain of the fleece. Using a ½-inch-wide seam allowance, sew the short ends of each strip together to make a circle. Trim the seam allowance to ¼ inch and press open.

9. With the seam at the vest underarm seam, pin and stitch a binding circle to each armhole using the procedure you used to bind the lower edge. ❖

Celtic Key Pattern
Enlarge 200 percent.

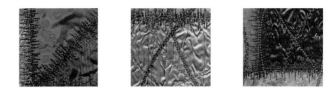

PATCHWORK PUZZLER

Design by Pat Nelson

First choose a simple pattern for a lined jacket in the style of your choice. Next choose your favorite fabrics in colors you love. Then cut them up and arrange them on the jacket foundation. And then read on to find out how simple it is to make a patchwork jacket without any piecing seams. It's easy and fun!

Finished Size
Your size

Techniques
Seamless patchwork
Couching

Materials
- Pattern for lined jacket in style of your choice; cut-on or dropped shoulder sleeves are ideal, as well as kimono and cardigan styles
- ½ yard each of at least 8 coordinating fabrics for the patchwork
- Lining fabric in yardage given on the pattern for your size
- 45-inch-wide lightweight fusible woven or sheer weft-insertion interfacing (see Note at right)
- All-purpose thread to match fabrics
- Bobbin thread (60/2 weight)
- Decorative rayon or polyester thread, or clear monofilament
- Variety of decorative fibers, braids or cords for embellishment
- Couching presser foot, or open-toe embroidery/appliqué presser foot
- Universal 80/12 sewing machine needles
- Topstitching 80/12 sewing machine needles
- Embroidery needle, size 75/11
- Darning foot
- *Optional:* Temporary Spray adhesive
- Rotary cutter, mat and ruler
- Press cloth
- Basic sewing tools and equipment

Note: *Lightweight fusible woven or weft-insertion interfacings are recommended for their natural stability and drape. Do not substitute nonwoven fusible interfacing.*

Cutting

- Immerse the fusible interfacing in a basin of hot water and allow the water to cool. When cool, gently squeeze out the water and hang the interfacing to dry over the shower rod.
- Wash and dry washable fabrics. Pretreat other fabric types for shrinkage in an appropriate manner—steaming or steam pressing with lots of steam at the appropriate heat is recommended for those that cannot be laundered.
- Adjust the pattern to fit your figure as needed.
- From the lining, cut the pattern pieces as instructed in the pattern.
- From the interfacing, cut the jacket fronts and back, and sleeves, if they are not cut on with the front and back. Cut each piece 1 inch beyond the cutting line at all edges to allow for a bit of shrinkage in the fusing and stitching process. You will trim to size later.
- Use a pencil to draw the straight of grain (transfer from the pattern pieces) on the resin (sticky) side of each piece of interfacing to use as an alignment guide for the patchwork squares and rectangles. Extend each grain line from the top to the bottom edge of the interfacing.
- Cut one 9-inch square from the leftover interfacing for a patchwork sampler.
- Cut the patchwork fabrics into 3-, 4- and 5-inch-wide strips, making the cuts parallel to the selvage. From these strips, cut an assortment of patchwork pieces (3-, 4- and 5-inch squares, and 3 x 4- and 3 x 5-inch rectangles). It is essential to cut these shapes accurately, so take your time. Separate the pieces into piles by color and size.

Note: If you prefer, you can cut all the pieces the same size and shape (squares or rectangles).

Assembly

1. On a large work surface, arrange the jacket front interfacing pieces side by side with the resin side facing up.

2. Using the grain line as a placement guide, randomly position the patchwork shapes face up on the interfacing, butting the edges so that no interfacing shows (Figure 1). Do not fuse in place until you are satisfied with the arrangement. If you have patches cut from napped fabrics, read the Note below first. Fuse following the manufacturer's directions, using a press cloth to protect the iron from picking up any fusible residue. Also see Note below before fusing.

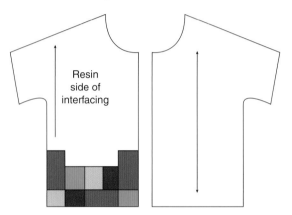

Figure 1
Arrange patchwork pieces on jacket fronts cut from fusible interfacing.

Note: If your fabric selection includes napped fabrics, temporarily remove them from their position on the interfacing while fusing the other pieces in place. Then apply a light coat of temporary spray adhesive to the wrong side of the napped pieces and position them on the interfacing. Use a cooler iron if fusing sheer or delicate fabrics.

3. Prepare the patchwork on the interfacing for the jacket back and the sleeves in the same manner.

4. Arrange leftover fabric pieces on the 9-inch square of interfacing and fuse in place. Use this as your practice piece to check out your thread and embellishment choices using the techniques described in the following steps before working on the jacket pieces.

5. Insert the topstitching needle in the machine and thread with two strands of decorative thread. Make sure that at least 50 percent of the eye of the needle is not filled with thread. If the thread is too heavy it will shred. Replace with a larger-size needle if necessary.

Note: Refer to the directions in your sewing machine manual for information on how to thread with two threads. For a machine with a spring tension, thread the two threads at the same time. For a machine with a tension disk, place the threads on opposite sides of the tension disks. Use bobbin thread in the bobbin.

6. Use the 9-inch sampler square to experiment with different threads and both techniques following the directions in Stitch It! on page 164, and then cover the raw edges of the patchwork on all of the garment pieces. Use the stitching method and threads you prefer. Press the finished pieces to eliminate any puckering.

7. Choose one or both of the following methods to further embellish the patchwork surface: random stitching and/or couching.
a. Using a variety of different threads, stitch random lines over the patchwork piece using a normal straight stitch and regular or decorative thread (Figure 2).

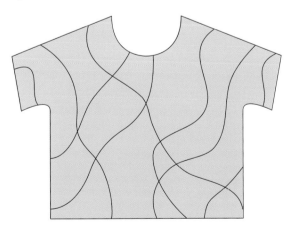

Figure 2
Add random stitching to each patchwork panel (patchwork not shown).

b. Couch thicker threads to the surface of each patchwork piece following Couch It! on page 165.

8. Replace the pattern pieces on the completed patchwork pieces and trim to size as needed.

9. Complete the jacket following the pattern guidesheet directions. ❖

Stitch It!

Cover all raw edges with free-motion stitching or with decorative stitching following the directions below.

Free-Motion Stitching

1. Attach the darning foot and lower the feed dogs.

2. Decrease the top thread tension so the bobbin thread is not pulled to the surface of your work as you stitch.

3. Set the stitch length and width at 0 for free-motion stitching.

4. Using an irregular, side-to-side motion, stitch back and forth over the butted raw edges. The stitches should bite into both fabrics and the resulting irregular stitching should be about ¼ inch wide (Figure 1). Stitch across all horizontally aligned edges first, and then stitch all verticals. Whenever you reach an outer edge, stop moving the fabric and stitch in place for several stitches to lock the stitching.

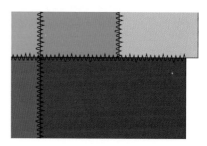

Figure 1
Use side-to-side free-motion stitch
to cover raw edges of patches.

Note: *If there are any gaps between the butted fabric edges, fill these areas with a few rows of free-motion stitching before covering them with the side-to-side stitching.*

Decorative Machine Stitching

1. Set up the machine as directed above.

2. Choose a decorative stitch with a wide zigzag and good coverage so that the raw edges will be well covered by the stitching.

Couch It!

Couching is a decorative stitching method for applying thicker threads that are too large to fit through the machine needle to a fabric surface.

• Contrasting, matching and invisible threads may be used for this technique.

• If available, you might want to invest in a special couching foot for your machine because it will eliminate some of the work.

• Look for thicker fibers such as metallic or rayon braid, pearl cotton size 3 or 5, crochet cotton or any other decorative cord that will complement your project. Don't overlook the offerings at cross-stitch and needlework shops.

• To couch thick fibers, use decorative rayon or polyester thread or clear monofilament thread in the needle, depending on the desired look.

• Couch with matching or contrasting thread colors as desired.

• Test the following technique on your 9-inch sampler square before couching the jacket pieces; adjust tensions and stitch width and length as needed.

1. Set up your machine for regular sewing and insert an embroidery needle, size 75/11. Adjust the machine for a balanced, narrow zigzag stitch that just clears the couching thread (Figure 1).

Figure 1
Trap trim under zigzagging
to couch to surface.

2. Attach the couching foot, if available, or substitute an open-toe embroidery/appliqué foot.

3. Thread the needle with your choice of decorative thread and the bobbin with bobbin thread.

4. If using a couching foot, refer to the directions that come with it to insert the couching thread. If using an open-toe foot, arrange the couching material on the fabric right side between the two toes of the foot.

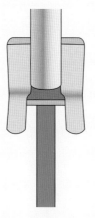

Figure 2
Position couching cord between
toes of open-toe presser foot.

Note: *If you are using cords and fibers of varying thicknesses, sew the thickest ones in place last to make the work easier, especially if you are applying beads or pearls (these require a special beading foot; check with your dealer).*

5. Beginning at a garment edge, stitch gentle curves up and down your garment pieces. Do an odd number of rows on each piece before switching to another couching cord if you are using two or more different ones.

6. After you are finished couching, press the garment pieces with steam to eliminate any puckering.

ASIAN CHEVRONS

Design by Barbara Weiland

Interlocking points and oriental prints create the patchwork panels in this simple cardigan. No need to shy away from the inside points in this pieced marvel when you follow this foolproof method.

Finished Size
Your size

Technique
Patchwork with inset corners

Materials
Project Note: *Jacket shown and yardage given is for a size medium cardigan-style jacket with a back length of approximately 29 inches, not including the stand-up, cut-on collar; smaller sizes and different styles may require less and larger sizes may require additional yardage for the chevrons.*
• Cardigan-style jacket pattern (no front overlap or buttons)
• 44/45-inch-wide cotton prints:
  ⅞ yard each 6 or 7 coordinating Asian prints (or other theme)
  ½ yard contrasting print or solid for binding
  Lightweight cotton flannel in the yardage listed for the jacket on the pattern envelope, plus ½ yard

Coordinating print or solid fabric for lining/foundation in yardage indicated on the pattern envelope, plus ½ yard
• ¼-inch presser foot
• All-purpose thread to blend with fabric colors
• Notions as directed on the pattern envelope
• Air- or water-soluble marking pen
• *Optional:* temporary spray adhesive
• *Optional:* approximately 5 yards narrow flexible braid trim
• Rotary cutter, mat and ruler
• Basic sewing tools and equipment

Cutting

- Preshrink all fabrics before you begin. Press to remove wrinkles and trim away the selvages.
- Measure the width of the fabrics. If your fabrics are not 42 inches wide at this point, you will probably need to cut an additional strip from each fabric in order to cut the required number of rectangles from each strip. It will depend on the jacket length and size. After creating the patchwork panels for the fronts, you will probably be able to determine if you will need additional rectangles.
- From each of at least six coordinating prints, for size medium and up, cut four 6 x 42-inch strips. Cut 6 x 10-inch rectangles from each strip. For smaller sizes, cut four strips each 5 x 42 inches and cut each strip into 5 x 10-inch rectangles. Depending on the size, style and length of your jacket, you may need to cut an additional strip from each fabric for additional rectangles. Determine this as you work through the patchwork design and assembly steps.

Note: Fold the rectangles in half lengthwise with wrong sides facing and raw edges even. Press lightly to create a center crease in each one. If you have cut the rectangles in a double layer, you can fold them together carefully rather than separating them for this step. Do not fold more than a double layer of rectangles to preserve accuracy.

- Position a folded rectangle on the rotary-cutting mat with the long raw edges even with the 45-degree-angle line and the corner at the cut edges located at the point of a square as shown in Figure 1.

Figure 1
Position folded rectangle with
raw edges along 45-degree line.

- Cut away the corner as shown in Figures 2a and 2b.

Figure 2a
Position ruler along line on mat that intersects
the upper corner of folded rectangle.

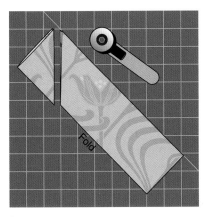

Figure 2b
Cut away corner triangle.

• Adjust the piece so the lower corner of the folded rectangle is at the intersection of two lines on the rotary-cutting mat and the cut edges are aligned with the 45-degree line. Cut away the corner (Figure 3).

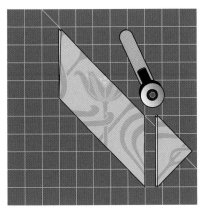

Figure 3
Cut away lower triangle.

• Open each rectangle to reveal a chevron (Figure 4). Discard the triangle cutaways or set aside for another patchwork project.

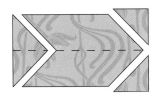

Figure 4
Open chevron and discard triangle cutaways (or save for another project).

• Repeat the above steps to cut chevrons from all remaining rectangles.

Note: *Do not press the rectangles to remove the center crease.*

• From the coordinating fabric for the lining/foundation, cut a rectangle large enough to accommodate each of the jacket pieces plus a little extra all around—two sleeves, two fronts and one back (Figure 5). Each rectangle should be slightly larger than the length and width of the pattern piece and cut on grain. Repeat with the lightweight cotton flannel.

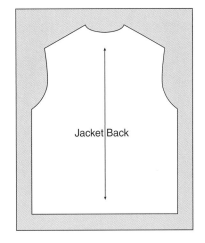

Figure 5
Cut a rectangle of lining for each jacket piece.

• From the binding fabric, cut five strips each 2½ inches wide, cutting across the fabric width.

Patchwork Assembly
Note: *Use ¼-inch-wide seam allowances for the patchwork.*

1. Adjust the stitch length on the sewing machine to 15 stitches per inch and attach the ¼-inch presser foot if available. If not, see Perfectly Pivoted Points on page 174.

2. Beginning and ending 1 inch from the inward point on each chevron, stitch exactly ¼ inch from the raw edge and pivot precisely at the pressed crease line.

Note: *Do not press to remove the crease line; you will need it to assist in positioning the pieces for perfect pivots at the points.*

Clip the threads and clip the inward corner of each chevron to within a thread of the stitching (Figure 6).

Figure 6
Stitch ¹/₄" from inward point and clip.

3. Draw a line ⅝ inch from the front edge of the jacket front pattern piece and trim away the pattern at this line; repeat at the back neckline edge. This eliminates the seam allowance, since you will be binding the edge instead of adding a facing.

4. Adjust the pattern to fit your figure before proceeding. Place the right front pattern piece face up on the work surface and arrange a row of chevrons along the front edge of the jacket pattern; use enough chevrons to completely cover the pattern from the upper to lower edge plus a few inches extra to allow for seaming loss when the pieces are sewn together. For most sizes and styles, each vertical row of patchwork will require five chevrons to adequately cover the length of the pattern pieces.

5. Add a second row of chevrons with the point in the opposite direction (see completed patchwork panels in Figure 8). Note that the upper and lower edges will be jagged. Add a third row of chevrons (necessary for most sizes from medium up) with the points in the same direction as in the first row. Pin the chevrons to the pattern tissue temporarily.

6. Move the right front pattern and the chevrons to your sewing machine or a location nearby so that you can sew the pieces together in each row to create the patchwork strips. Remove the pins, leaving the chevrons in the established positions.

7. Working on one row of chevrons at a time, follow the directions for Perfectly Pivoted Points on page 174 to join the chevrons; press all seams toward the outward points in each strip. Replace the completed strips in position on the pattern piece.

8. Sew the chevron rows together for the right jacket front, taking care to match the chevron seams at each ¼-inch seam intersection where they cross. Return the pattern piece with patchwork strips to the work surface, and check the upper areas to make sure that the entire pattern piece is covered. If necessary, add another chevron to the upper end of the row where needed. You will need to undo a bit of the vertical seam to add the extra chevron and then restitch (Figure 7).

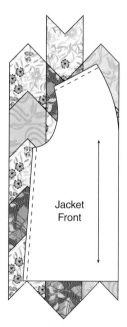

Figure 7
Check pattern on completed patchwork panel. Add chevrons if needed to accomodate pattern.

9. Arrange chevrons on the wrong side of the jacket front pattern piece in a mirror-image arrangement of the right front patchwork panel you just completed. Sew the chevrons together in rows and sew the rows together as you did for the right front (Figure 8). Set the completed front panels aside.

Figure 8
Mirror-Image Panels for Jacket Fronts

10. Working on the sleeve pattern piece, create the chevron rows for the sleeve as you did for the jacket fronts. This time, though, begin with a row for the center of the sleeve, and then add the required number of rows at each side of the center row. Most sleeves will require three rows of chevron strips. Press the long seams toward the underarm edges (Figure 9).

Press.

Figure 9
Sleeve Panel.
Make 2.

11. Repeat the process for the jacket back, creating five rows of chevron strips with the first one centered over the center-back line on the jacket. Sew the strips together when you are sure they are long enough to entirely cover the back pattern piece. Press all seams away from the center strip of chevrons toward the side seam edges (Figure 10).

Center-Back Crease

Press.

Figure 10
Back Panel.
Make 1.

12. Apply a light coat of temporary spray adhesive to the wrong side of one rectangle of lightweight flannel for the jacket front, and smooth the adhesive-coated side onto the wrong side of a matching lining rectangle. Repeat with the remaining rectangles for each of the jacket pieces.

13. Apply a light coat of temporary spray adhesive to the wrong side of each patchwork panel and smooth in place on top of the flannel. Check the vertical seam lines and make sure they are parallel to the straight-grain edge of the rectangle. Use a long rotary ruler to help with this step. If you prefer not to use the spray adhesive, carefully arrange the three layers, smooth out wrinkles, align the vertical seam lines, and then place straight pins across the vertical seam lines to secure the layers for the next step.

14. Stitch in the ditch of all vertical seams to attach the patchwork to the flannel and the lining in one step. Stitch in the ditch of all remaining seams of the patchwork that cross the vertical lines (Figure 11).

Figure 11
Stitch in the ditch of vertical seams,
and then the zigzag seams.

15. Repeat the above steps to apply the patchwork panels to their corresponding layers of flannel and lining and add trim if desired.

Jacket Cutting & Assembly

1. Position the pattern pieces on the panels and cut out. When cutting the jacket fronts, place the lower edge along the inward points of the chevrons as shown in Figure 7 on page 170. Take care to match the chevron seam lines at the center front and be sure to cut a right and left front (Figure 12).

Note: For best results, cut the right front first and then remove the pattern piece. Place the right front facedown on the remaining front patchwork panel, matching chevron points throughout and especially at the front edge to ensure that the chevrons will line up

straight across the jacket fronts in the finished jacket. Cut the left front.

Figure 12
Cut jacket fronts from patchwork panels.

2. When cutting the back, place the lower edge at the inward points of the patchwork panel and position the center-back fold at the center of the middle of the strip of chevrons. Cut the first half, and then flip the pattern piece to cut the remaining half of the back (Figure 13).

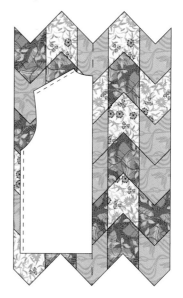

Figure 13
Position back pattern piece along center-back
crease. Cut first half; flip pattern to cut second half.

3. Center the sleeve on the patchwork panel and position the pattern piece so the chevrons will line up across the sleeves and jacket front and back as closely as possible (Figure 14). Cut out one sleeve. Flip the cutout sleeve facedown onto the remaining patchwork panel and line up vertical and horizontal zigzag seam lines before cutting.

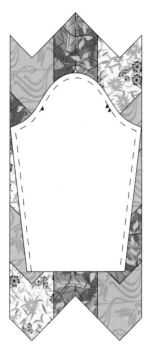

Figure 14
Position sleeve on patchwork panel
with shoulder dot at center crease.

4. Sew the jacket side and shoulder seams and insert the sleeves following the pattern guidesheet directions. Press the shoulder and side seams open and finish seam edges with serging or a Hong Kong finish as shown on page 33 for the Paint 'n' Fuse jacket.

5. Try on the jacket and turn up the lower edges of the sleeve and jacket to the desired finished lengths. Pin in place, and then press and remove the pins. Cut away the hem allowances to prepare for the binding.

6. Sew the 2½-inch-wide binding strips together using bias seams to make one long strip. Press the seams open.

7. Fold the binding strip in half lengthwise with wrong sides facing and raw edges aligned; press. Use the strip to bind all raw edges of the jacket. Stitch to the right side with a ⅜-inch-wide seam. Press the binding toward the seam allowance and turn to the inside. Hand-stitch in place or pin in place and stitch in the ditch from the right side. Miter corners as you reach them.

8. *Optional: If desired, position flexible braid trim along the inner edge of the binding and stitch in place. Outline the sleeve seam in the same manner.* ❖

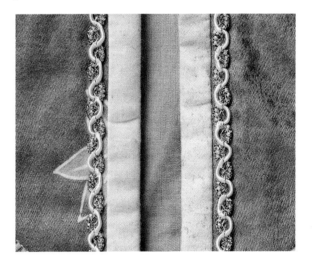

Perfectly Pivoted Points

1. Working on one row of chevrons at a time, arrange a pair as shown with the folded edge of the top chevron perpendicular to the crease in the lower chevron. Note that a small triangle extends at the long edge of the lower chevron (Figure 1).

Figure 1
Position folded rectangle
on point of lower chevron.

2. Carefully unfold the top chevron without disturbing the positioning and pin in place at each end. Stitch as shown in Figure 2, taking a few backstitches at the inside corner of the chevron. Clip the threads and remove the work from the machine (Figure 2).

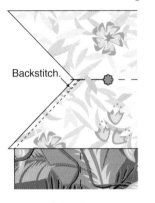

Figure 2
Unfold top chevron and pin.
Stitch just to crease; backstitch.

3. Arrange the second half of the seam and pin. Stitch, beginning at the inward point and taking a few backstitches before continuing to the end of the seam (Figure 3).

Figure 3
Sew second half of seam to remaining edge.

4. Continue adding chevrons in this manner to complete the row, and then take the strip to the ironing board. Press all seams toward the outward point in each row; press carefully to remove the center crease in each chevron (Figure 4).

Figure 4
Press chevron seams toward points.

Fabric & Supplies

Page 126: *Angel Felt*—Angelina fibers from joggles.com (Internet orders only); Timtex heavyweight nonwoven stabilizer available from The Timtex Store.

Page 110: *Bleach Play*—Clorox Bleach Pen Gel; Waverly Fabrics.

Page 18: *Boldly Stitched*—12-weight cotton embroidery thread from Sulky of America; Husqvarna Viking Disk 69, Geometric Sensations; The Warm Co. Steam-A-Seam2 paper-backed fusible web.

Page 149: *Circle Up!*—Sewing machine provided by by Husqvarna Viking Sewing Machines.

Page 40: *Foiled Again!*—Metallic foils and adhesive from Laura Murray Designs.

Page 88: *Heartfelt Chenille*—½-inch V-effect Chenille the Easy Way tissues from CASU Design.

Page 78: *Irresistible Garden*—Scribbles Dimensional Fabric Paint by Duncan: glittering gold and silver; Jacquard Lumiere Light Body Metallic Acrylic #565 metallic bronze; The Warm Co. Lite Steam-A-Seam2 paper-backed fusible web.

Page 134: *A Jeans Affair*—The Warm Co. Steam-A-Seam2 paper-backed fusible web; threads from Sulky of America; crystals from Creative Crystal Co.; Shiva Artist Paintstiks available at Blick Art Materials; brushes Loew-Cornell.

Page 24: *Make Mine Confetti*—DMC rayon embroidery thread; Kreinik Mfg. Co. Inc. decorative metallic threads; The Warm Co. Lite Steam-A-Seam2 paper-backed fusible web; Kandi Corp. Hot-Fix Light and emerald fusible crystals, and L'orna Hot Fix Swarovski fusible crystals; buttons from Blumenthal Lansing Co.

Page 83: *Oh, What Relief!*—Construction and decorative embroidery threads from Coats & Clark; monofilament thread from YLI Corp.

Page 28: *Paint 'N' Fuse*—Getting to the Point Jacket by Saf-T-Pockets Patterns, SoSoft Fabric Acrylics paint by DecoArt; Scribbles Dimensional Fabric Paint by Duncan; The Warm Co. Lite Steam-A-Seam2 paper-backed fusible web; decorative threads from Sulky of America.

Page 34: *Put It in Your Piping*—12-weight cotton embroidery thread from Sulky of America; Crafter's Choice Pillow Insert from Fairfield; The Ultimate! Glue from Crafter's Pick; Embroidery Resource All-over and Everywhere embroidery CD; The Warm Co. Steam-A-Seam2 paper-backed fusible web.

Page 121: *Stitch It With Twins*—The Warm Co. Steam-A-Seam2 paper-backed fusible web; Madeira sewing and embroidery threads.

Page 51: *Stamped & "Hole-y"*—Eyelet Appeal Jacket #IJ727 from Indygo Junction; fabrics by Waverly Fabrics; buttons from Incomparable Buttons; eyelets, grommets and pliers from Prym Dritz; Purrfectly Clear Art Stamps, Jacquard Textile Paint and paint stamp pad from Purrfection Artistic Wearables.

Page 98: *Twist & Stitch*—Spinster available from www.clotilde.com.

Page 106: *Velvet Wrap-Ture*—Dharma Trading Co. dye-ready fabrics and dyes.

Sewing Sources

The following companies provided fabric and/or supplies for projects in this book. If you are unable to locate a product locally, contact the manufacturers listed below for the closest retail or mail-order source.

API Crafter's Pick
(510) 526-7616
www.crafterspick.com

Beacon Adhesives
(914) 699-3400
www.beaconcreates.com

Blick Art Materials
(800) 828-4548
www.dickblick.com

Blumenthal Lansing Co.
(563) 538-4211
www.buttonsplus.com

CASU Design
(604) 945-3007
www.casudesign.com

Clorox Bleach Co.
www.clorox.com

Coats & Clark
(800) 648-1479
www.coatsandclark.com

Creative Crystal Co.
(800) 578-0716
www.creative-crystal.com

DecoArt
(800) 367-3047
www.decoart.com

Dharma Trading Co.
(800) 542-5227
www.dharmatrading.com

DMC Corp.
(973) 589-0606, ext. 3046
www.dmc-usa.com

Duncan Enterprises
(800) 438-6226
www.duncancrafts.com

Embroidery Resource
(800) 953-7656
www.embroideryresource.com

Fairfield
(800) 980-8000
www.poly-fil.com

Husqvarna Viking USA
(800) 358-0001
www.husqvarnaviking.com/us/

Indygo Junction
(913) 341-5559
www.indygojunction.com

Jacquard Products
(800) 442-0455
www.jacquardproducts.com

Joggles.com
(401)398-2657
www.joggles.com

Kandi Corp.
(800) 985-2634
www.kandicorp.com

Kreinik
(800) 537-2166
www.kreinik.com

Laura Murray Designs
www.lauramurraydesigns.com

Loew-Cornell
(201) 836-7070
www.loew-cornell.com

Madiera USA
www.madierausa.com
available at: SCS USA
19018 E. Portal Way
Portland, OR 97230

Mokuba New York
(212) 869-8900
www.mokubany.com

Prym Consumer USA Inc.
www.dritz.com

Purrfection Artistic Wearables
(800) 691-4293
www.purrfection.com

Saf-T-Pockets Patterns
(503) 761-6460
www.saf-t-pockets.com

Sulky of America
(800) 874-4115
www.sulky.com

Toray Ultrasuede America
www.ultrasuede.com

The Timtex Store
(208) 664-2664
www.timtexstore.com

The Warm Co.
(800) 234-WARM
www.warmcompany.com

Waverly Fabrics
www.waverly.com

YLI Corp.
(803) 985-3106
www.ylicorp.com

Special Thanks

We would like to thank the talented sewing designers whose work is featured in this collection.

Pam Archer
Circle Up!, 149
Velvet Wrap-Ture, 106

Diane Bunker
A Jeans Affair, 134

Stephanie Corina Goddard
Beaded Shrug, 13
Bead Toss, 46

Lucy B. Gray
Alphabet Soup, 6
Angel Felt, 126
Button Faces, 114
Crazy for Crayons, 68
Foiled Again!, 40
Metal-Some Stitching, 140
Sweetly Felted, 57

Linda Turner Griepentrog
Boldly Stitched, 18
Put It in Your Piping, 34

Carol Moffatt
Double Up, 154
Heartfelt Chenille, 88

Patsy Moreland
Irresistible Garden, 78
Make Mine Confetti, 24

Pat Nelson
Oh, What Relief!, 83
Patchwork Puzzler, 160
Twist & Stitch, 98

Pauline Richards
Graphic Punch, 63
Stitch It With Twins, 121

Lynn Weglarz
Paint 'n' Fuse, 28

Barbara Weiland
Asian Chevrons, 166

Carol Zentgraf
Bleach Play, 110
Ribbon Twists, 94
Stamped & "Hole-y", 51